THE HIDDEN WORLD
Number 10
THE SHAVER MYSTERY

Richard S. Shaver

R. B. Hoag

Ray Palmer

Timothy Green Beckley

This revised edition and new cover art
Copyright © 2011
Timothy Green Beckley
DBA Global Communications, All Rights Reserved

Originally Published by Palmer Publications, Summer 1963 A-10

No part of this book may be reproduced, stored in retrieval system or transmitted in any form or by any means, electronic, mechanical, photocopying, recording, without express permission of the publisher.

Timothy Green Beckley: Editorial
Director Carol Rodriguez: Publishers
Assistant Sean Casteel: Associate Editor
William Kern: Editorial Assistant
Cover Art: Tim Swartz

Printed in the United States of
America For free catalog write:
Global Communications
P.O. Box 753
New Brunswick, NJ 08903

Free Subscription to Conspiracy Journal E-Mail
Newsletter www.conspiracyjournal.com

Note: The four digit numbers at the bottom of each page indicates page number of the entire The Hidden World series. Below that is the page number of this individual book.

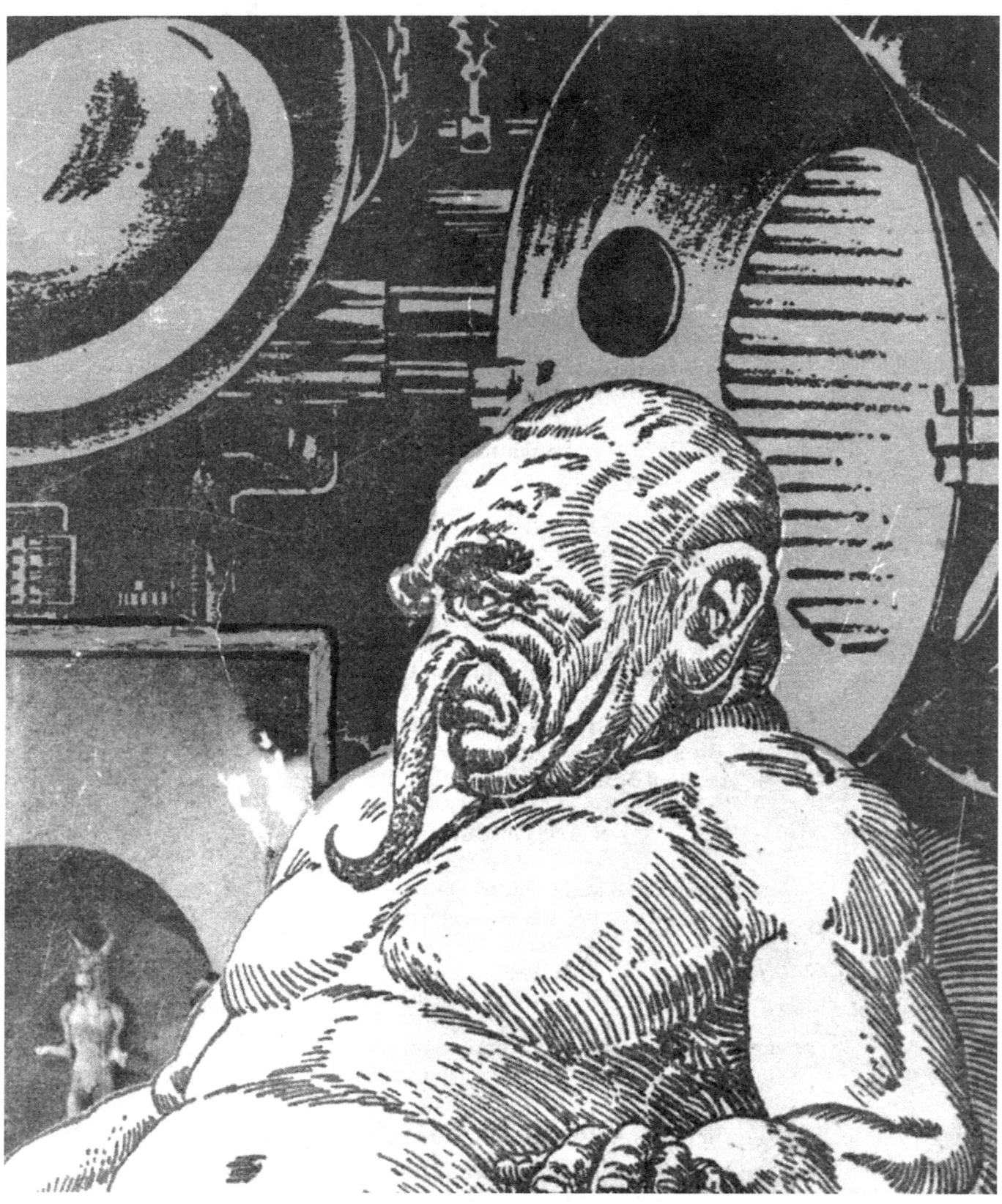

Hidden Worlds No. 10

Introduction To The New Edition of Hidden World No. 10

By
Timothy Green Beckley

Reading through the reprints of the Hidden World series has been an incredible experience. Originating in **Amazing Stories** back in the 1940s, the Shaver Mystery has had a long run, much longer than any TV show or comic book superhero.

Publisher Ray Palmer obviously had no way of knowing how he would be opening the flood gates to a mad house when he published Shaver's original piece, "I Remember Lemuria." Though he might pretend to, Palmer obviously had no way of knowing that this eccentric welder at the Ford Motor company would soon be attacked for his beliefs by the die hard skeptics on one hand, and supported so strongly on the other by die hard believers.

Shaver's descriptions of a hellish underworld inhabited by the Dero with their ancient mind control equipment stirred the public's imagination, but was it really their imagination he was stirring or a subliminal memory of an ancient world gone totally mad due to the radioactive rays of the sun?

We will never know for sure, but there is still a great interest in the topics Shaver discussed as if these were topics that were part of our daily news feeds. That is why we are so exuberant over the new cache of "lost" articles by Shaver which we started publishing in the last issue and will continue with throughout the rest of the series.

We received these stories through the Shaver Mystery Yahoo Group, an e mail chain letter group we actively participate in, exchanging hundreds of posts with other members on a regular basis. The group is very ably moderated by Richard Toronto from whom you can find out more by simply going to www.ShaverTron.Com. If you have things in common with the stated purpose of the group you will be welcome to join.

This issue we are proud to present the "lost" Shaver story entitled "The Plotters." – well yes our world is controlled and now you can find out what Shaver had to say on this ever captivating subject.

And if you notice a bit of "distortion" on a couple of the pages, please accept our formal apologies. Due to the nature and age of the original manuscript there might be what we call in printer's lingo a bit of offset feedback on several of the sheets where the printing actually shows through from the other side of the paper. Our capable printer has attempted to remedy this situation as much as possible.

All things considered, we are attempting as best we can to save all Sixteen Volumes of **Hidden World** so that there will be a record of Shaver's claims for generations to come. The original paper stock was very pulpish and the print has started to fade with the decades, and the pages themselves have started to get frayed and ripped as they stay longer in the hands of collectors.

So let us tip our hat and raise our drinking glass to the heroes of our stories who have created a fabulous genera be it science fact or science fiction. Read on dear friends. Please read on!

Timothy G Beckley
www.ConspiracyJournal.Com

Hidden Worlds No. 10

The Plotters

By Richard S. Shaver

***

He came from a far planet to find some of the Earth's secrets. But Marko found other things, too; like his love for beautiful Beth.

***

IT SEEMED to be the same tree that kept getting in my way. I tried to go around it but it moved with me and I ran right into it. I found myself sprawled on my back and my nose was bleeding where I had hit it against the tree. Then I got up and ran again.

I had to keep running. I didn't know why; I just had to. There was a puddle of water and I splashed through it and then slipped and fell into a thorny bush. When I got up there were scratches on my hands and face and chest.

As yet I felt no pain. That wouldn't come for a while, after I had done a lot more running. But at the moment I couldn't feel a thing.

In my conscious mind there was only a sort of grayness. I didn't know where I was, or who I was, or why I was running. I didn't know that if I ran long enough and bumped into enough trees and scratched myself often enough I would eventually feel pain. Or that out of the exertion and the pain would come awareness.

All that must have been there, but buried so deep it didn't come through. It was only instinct which kept me going.

The same tree was in my way again and this time I didn't even try to go around it. My breath was knocked out of me. After a few gasps it came back, and then I was off again.

I went up a rise and down into a hollow and tripped over roots. That time I didn't fall. I went up the other side of the hollow with the wind whistling in my ears. A few drops of rain fell. There were flashes of lightning in the sky.

Wet leaves whipped against my face and there was a crack of thunder so close that it shook me. I ran away from the thunder and up another rise and down into another hollow.

The wind was stronger now. It came in long blasts. Sometimes I ran with it and sometimes against it. When I ran against it I didn't make much headway, but my legs kept pumping. There was tall grass to slow me down and there were roots to trip me. There was the wind and the thunder and the lightning. And there were always trees.

And then there was a terrible flash and above me a crack that was not of thunder. Something came crashing down. It was the limb of a tree. It crashed against my chest and smashed me flat on my back and pinned me there.

One of my ribs felt broken. It jabbed into me as I fought to raise this weight from my chest, and this was a pain I could feel.

This was something that hurt as nothing had ever hurt me before. This was excruciating. But it was the pain that cut through the grayness of my mind, and because of that I welcomed it.

I was Marko. I knew that much already. Beth was the golden girl. Somehow I knew that too. But who were the others?

It wasn't coming fast enough. I couldn't find the connections. There was only one way to bring it back, to bridge the gaps. I had to start somewhere, with what I knew. I had to start with myself and then bridge the gap to Beth. That was the beginning.

I CHECKED with the mirror for the last time and decided that I would pass muster. As far as I could see, I looked like almost any college student.

There wasn't anything I could do about my hair. It hadn't grown at all. It was a mass of short, black ringlets that fit my head like a tight cap. But there was no use worrying about that.

Mrs. Mara came down the hall just as I was locking the door. She looked hurt when she saw me turn the key.

"You don't have to do that in my house," she said. "There's nobody would think of going into your room."

"Of course not," I said. "It's just force of habit, you know."

I smiled and hoped she would pass it off as lightly as I seemed to. The last thing in the world I wanted was to have her get suspicious and go prowling about my room. I felt easier when she smiled back at me.

"Sure. And where are you off to, now?"

"Swimming," I said. "That is, if I can get into the college pool."

"Just act like you own the place and nobody will ask you any questions," she said, and winked at me.

That was exactly the way I had figured it, but it was good to have reassurance. Theoretically, no one was supposed to use the pool who was not a member of the faculty or student body. Enforcement, however, was lax, and the chances were that nobody would ask to see my card.

Mrs. Mara and I were right. The day was hot, and the men who were supposed to be watching the entrance were sitting in the shade of the stands and quenching their thirst with soft drinks. I walked right in, looking straight ahead.

It was a large pool, used for skating in winter, and there were stands built on three sides. Instead of going down to the locker rooms, I merely slipped out of my shirt and trousers, rolled them into a ball and dropped them beside the pool. A good many others had also worn their swim suits underneath. Then I looked around for the girl.

SHE WAS down near the other end of the pool, talking to some people. As I came toward them she left the group and climbed up on the diving board.

Against her white bathing suit, her small trim figure showed golden. Her hair was almost the same color. She looked like the bathing suit models I had seen in store windows. The golden model came to life as she left the board in a high, arching dive. She hit the water with hardly a splash.

"Was it really, Ken?" the girl asked.

He nodded as he said it was. They began to talk about diving and swimming. The man called Ken did most of the talking. He said he wanted to show her a few things about her swimming stroke.

He jumped off the edge of the pool and swam across and then turned around and swam back. Everybody stopped what they were doing and watched him. When he clambered out he smiled in a very superior way.

"See what I mean? You've got to use your legs more."

"You splash too much," I said.

It was the only way I could think of at the moment to get into the conversation. But it got me in.

Everybody was looking at me as though I were out of my mind. Ken sneered.

"Oh, I do?"

"Don't take it offensively," I said. "But you really do. Also your arm motion is not good."

HE WAS so angry that it was almost funny. Now I was sorry I had spoken, because the girl might be a close friend of his and she might take offense.

"Maybe you would like to show me how it's done," Ken said hotly. "I could make it worth your while. Suppose we race two lengths. For ten dollars."

"That's not fair, Ken," the girl said. I could see that she didn't like the way he was taking it, so that was all right. But I hesitated. I didn't have ten dollars. On the other hand, I had been watching these people swim.

It was an easy way to make ten dollars, since I had no other means of getting money. There was the hundred dollars which I had taken from a man on the road the day I came into town, but that money was gone.

"Come on," I said, and started walking to the end of the pool.

When I got there I bent and dipped one foot into the water. It was colder than the water I had been used to, and not quite as heavy, somehow. I pulled my foot out quickly and everybody laughed, except the girl.

"This isn't right," she said. She turned to me. "You don't know who Ken is, apparently."

"You are very kind," I said. I smiled at her and she smiled back. She had blue eyes.

By that time the pool had been cleared. Everybody was out of the water and standing at the edge. Ken said, "Whenever you're ready."

"I am ready now," I said. And immediately one of his friends gave the signal, "Go!"

Ken jumped in first. Then I dived in. Once in the water it did not feel so cold nor so light. I swam down to the other end and turned around and swam back. When I climbed out, Ken was just making his turn at the far end. Everyone was looking at me very strangely. Ken came out rubbing his shoulder.

"Must have pulled a muscle," he muttered.

"I don't believe I've seen you around before," he said. "You've got to have a card to swim here, you know."

"Well, I don't have one. So I suppose I had better go."

"Of all the cheap tricks," the girl said. "I think I'll go too. Wait for me."

I waited for her while she went to get dressed. I put on my trousers over my swimming trunks, put on my shirt and shoes and sat on a bench and waited. When she came out we started for the exit. Ken came hurrying toward us.

"I thought I was taking you home," he said, his face red with anger.

She didn't bother to reply and he put his hand on her arm. I told him to let go and he let go. Then he swung around and hit me on the jaw with all his might. I grabbed his arm with one hand and his throat with the other and threw him into the middle of the pool.

THINGS were going better than I expected. As we walked along, she seemed quite interested in me. I told her my name and she told me that she was Beth Copperd, the daughter of a professor at the university. I pretended that I had not known those things.

When we got to her home, which was on a tree lined street, we paused for a moment. Across the street there was a car with a man sitting in it, pretending to read a newspaper.

I knew all about that man. I knew there was another man who was watching the back of the house. If not for that I would not have had to go through this lengthy affair with Beth Copperd.

"I regret very much this trouble with your friend," I said.

"You needn't. He's had it coming for a long time." She stared at me thoughtfully. "You know, Marko, I'm a little afraid of you."

"Of me? But why?"

"Well," she hesitated, "its hard to say. But when a man jumps into a pool and swims so much faster than one of our country's best swimmers, and then picks up that swimmer and throws him fifty feet without the slightest effort... well, that man is slightly unusual, to say the least."

"Oh, the swimming..."

I hadn't thought that what was quite ordinary for me might seem exactly the opposite to these people. I had blundered. So I tried to shrug it off, as though such things were common among my people. Which they were. But that line only dragged me deeper. This girl was no fool.

"That's what I meant, Marko. You aren't being modest. You're acting as though you're used to such feats, and take them as a matter of course. And there's your accent. I can't quite place it."

"Some day I'll tell you all about it." I said lightly. "When we know each other better."

"That's going pretty fast, isn't it?"

"Some of us have found that we don't have all the time we should like. We must go fast, or not at all."

It was a platitude, slightly jumbled, but none the less true. Beth was looking up at me. There were things she might have noticed; that my skin was uncommonly smooth, and that I hadn't even the faintest trace of whiskers.

"Will you come in for a while?" she asked slowly.

I relaxed. Everything was all right, for the present. She was taking me at face value. She liked me and I liked her. The operation was proceeding smoothly. We walked into a large room, pleasantly furnished. On a couch opposite the doorway three men sat talking. Two others stood before them. The moment we entered, the conversation stopped abruptly.

"Beth?" said a tall, graying man. He was already stuffing papers into a bag. "Back so soon?"

He wasn't really listening for a reply and Beth didn't make one. When he had the papers in the bag he locked it, then snapped it around his wrist and put the key in his pocket. "We'll continue this at the lab," he said to the men. "I'll be along in just a few minutes." Then he came up to us.

"I see you've replaced your blond young man," he smiled.

I knew all about this man who stood before me, with his stooped shoulders and keen eyes. Eldeth Copperd would have been surprised at the extent of my knowledge. I even knew why his government considered it wise to have several of its security agents near him at all times.

"Can't you stay a minute and get acquainted with Marko?" Beth was saying. "He's really a remarkable fellow. He can swim faster than you or I could run."

"Literally? That would be quite fast."

"Literally."

He looked at me with sudden interest and I was sorry the conversation had taken that turn. I didn't want those keen eyes examining me too closely. They might note the absence of skin porosity.

Copperd didn't notice, but I made a mental note to watch my step. And another not to go swimming again. Beth would be watching me, and if she were close enough she might see the webbing pop out between my fingers and toes when I got into the water.

"That's my father," Beth said after he and I had shaken hands and he had left. "Demands exactness. He's a scientist, you know. A physicist."

"Oh?" I said. As if I hadn't known. "Is he always this busy?"

"Busier. If he isn't working at the lab till all hours, he's working at home in his study. Or having conferences. The only time I have him alone and to myself is Sunday evening."

That was the information I had been hoping for.

BETH and I sat on the couch her father had vacated. We talked. I watched my words carefully; there were a good many commonplace things I knew nothing about. And I didn't want any more questions about myself. Fortunately, conversation between a young man and a young woman is much the same everywhere. I didn't have to pretend I was interested in Beth. She was unusually attractive. And she seemed to find me so. We talked a bit, laughed a good deal, and when I got up to leave I knew that I had done well in the

"May I see you tonight?" I asked. "Just a `coke date'."

That was an expression I'd heard and had taken the trouble to make certain I understood. It seemed to be just the thing in the present case.

"I'd like that," Beth said. "Pick me up about nine."

Her choice of time could not have been more suitable. I was out of money. There was Mrs. Mara to be paid, and now the cost of the evening's entertainment.

Until darkness fell I could do nothing about that. So I went back to my room and read old newspapers I had collected. I had discovered on my first day that those were the best sources of information. Those and the moving pictures.

For one who must learn a great deal about a people in a short time there is one infallible way: watch them in their favorite sports and relaxations. The moving pictures and the comic strips had been invaluable. In another few weeks I could have passed anywhere.

At eight o'clock it was growing dark. I changed my shirt, put on a sport coat and left the room. Five minutes later I was walking down a quiet street that was lined with fashionable homes.

After that it was merely a question of time. I went around the block, found that it was still too light, and went around again, this time slowly.

There was only one man on the street on my next time around. I sized him up quickly and decided that he was prosperous. He came on toward me. I managed to be looking the other way.

We bumped into each other and he fell. I said, "Sorry" and bent to help him up. My fingers touched his throat in the proper places and he went limp.

Within a matter of seconds I had his wallet out of his pocket and extracted several bills. When his eyes flickered again I was just raising him to his feet.

"All my fault," I said contritely. "Are you all right?"

"Seem to be." He was gruff, but that was all. He didn't know that for a matter of seconds he had been unconscious.

At nine o'clock I came up the walk to the Copperd home. This time the security agent was leaning against a tree, lighting a cigarette. I made certain that he saw my face clearly.

One upstairs window showed a light, and the faint murmur of voices drifted down. That had to be Copperd's room. Then a porch light flashed on and Beth came out of the door. She was wearing a white dress and the overhead light seemed to create a golden halo above her head.

I momentarily forgot about her father.

HOW much can a man learn in a few weeks? I had to be so very careful. Historical matters had to be avoided at all costs. Contemporary affairs were fine. Philosophy was best.

Philosophy is always the best. Good and evil are present everywhere. They can be discussed in the vaguest terms. We discussed many things in vague terms.

When I took her home I knew that it was not fear of the dark that made her walk so close to me. The movies had taught me a great deal about this matter of love play. Although some of it was highly exaggerated, it showed clearly enough the drives of these people, and some of their methods of acting them out.

We were standing on the porch when I kissed Beth. It was the first time I had ever pressed my lips to those of anyone else. My technique was good. I felt Beth respond, pressing harder against me.

My mission was on its way to completion. I felt a moment of triumph. And then suddenly, crazily, my mission was gone from my mind. I felt only a strange exhilaration that swept over me and made my heart pound and my head grow hot.

"What's the matter, Marko?" Beth asked as I pulled away.

I didn't know what was wrong. I didn't try to figure it out. I had to get out of there and try to regain my equilibrium. On a mission like mine I had to keep my head. "Shall I see you tomorrow?" I said. "All the tomorrow's you want," Beth answered.

There was eagerness, and yet a note of regret. It was as though she instinctively knew that something was wrong. But my work had been well done; she was in too far, and I had cut her emotional line of retreat.

I saw Beth the next afternoon, and the next evening. My presence on the porch and in her home became such a common thing that the security agent hardly gave me a glance now.

Those few days passed by swiftly, and yet each hour in those days was long. I was very cautious; Beth and I kissed many times but I never allowed myself to be moved as on that first time.

Sunday loomed larger and larger, closer and closer. I was a constant and ever present guest. It was an elementary matter to get Beth to invite me for Sunday dinner. The invitation came on Saturday night, and that night when I came back to my room I called Ristal for the first time since we had arrived. "Tomorrow," I said into the besnal. "Early evening."

"Good."

That was all we said, but it was enough. Our frequency was too high to be picked up. Still, we were taking no chances. Ristal knew precisely what I meant and he would be ready.

I had the feeling that comes when a mission is about to be completed. There was a feeling of tension, and yet for the first time in my career I had a lowering of spirits that I could not explain.

The feeling persisted until late Sunday afternoon. Then I pushed it from my mind. I dressed carefully, slipped the besnal into my inner pocket, and put my del gun in my coat pocket.

"Take your coat off," Beth said when I came in. "You ought to know there's no formality here."

"I'm really quite comfortable," I told her. "Am I late?"

"No. Just on time. Dad will be down in a moment."

He came down the stairs from his study while we were talking. He greeted me warmly, and yet I felt that this time he was scrutinizing me. All during the dinner his eyes were on me, weighing me. I felt what was coming, and as we rose from the table it came. "I hope you won't be offended, Marko," Copperd said. "But there are some strange things about

"No," I said. I looked out the window and saw it was growing darker.

"That's odd. And about your hair— have you ever realized that every strand of it grows in a different direction? You could never comb it. Your skin is of an unusually fine texture. And when you reached for something at the table I observed strange folds of skin between your fingers. You are somehow not like the rest of us."

"Naturally," I said. It didn't matter now. It was dark enough.

"Why naturally?"

"Because," I told him, "I am a Venusian."

MY TONE was matter of fact. Yet they knew that I was not joking. Beth was staring at me, a growing fear and horror in her eyes. Her father seemed dazed by the revelation. I took the del gun from my pocket and showed it to them.

"This is a weapon strange to you. But it is effective at this range. Please don't make me use it."

"But what do you want?" Copperd asked.

"I want you to take a ride with me. In your car."

I let them put on their coats and then we walked out onto the porch and down the stairs. Across the street the security agent barely glanced at us. Then we got into Copperd's car, Beth and he in the front seat and I in the back. I told him in which direction to go.

At the outskirts of town we lost the car that was following us. I had planned this part of it perfectly. We pulled into a side road and turned off our lights. The agent went right past us.

"What is it you want of me?" Copperd said as we started up again.

"We want to have a long discussion with you about some matters on which you are an authority."

"And that's what this whole affair with me was for? So that you could get to my father!" Beth said accusingly. I saw her shoulders shake.

"Yes. Now turn off here."

We turned off the main road and followed a rutted trail onto an old farm.

The farmhouse was a wreck, but the barn still good. Our ship was in there.

The door opened as we walked toward the barn. Ristal's tall figure was framed in the doorway, and behind him stood Kresh, broad and ungainly. The others crowded up behind them.

"Good work, Marko," Ristal said. We went into the ship, which filled the whole interior of the barn.

"This is Commander Ristal, of the Venusian Intelligence," I told Copperd and Beth.

"What's your official title?" Beth asked bitterly.

"I am a special agent and language expert," I told her. Then I explained why I had brought them here.

"I am a special agent and language expert," I told her. Then I explained why I had brought them here.

"When it became known that Earth was developing monstrous weapons of aggression we realized that we must be prepared for the worst. There was only one way to discover what you already had and what you were working on. Once we arrived here we found that a man named Copperd was the prime figure in his country's atomic weapons research. It became our duty to seek him out."

"I see," Copperd grunted. "And now you expect me to reveal secrets which I am bound by oath to

protect with my very life?"

"You will reveal them," Ristal told him.

I didn't like the way Ristal said that. There was a tinge of cruelty in his tone and in the sudden tightening of his lips. I hadn't ever worked with him before, or with Kresh, who was Ristal's second in command, but I didn't like the methods their manner implied. Copperd looked worried.

"I told you we were a peaceful people," I put in.

"Let me handle this," Ristal said. He pointed to a machine which stood in a corner.

"That," he explained to Copperd, "is a device which we ordinarily use in surgery and diagnosis. It has the faculty of making the nerves infinitely more sensitive to stimuli. Also to pain. Do you understand?"

"You can't use that on him!" I said. Ristal looked at me strangely.

"Of course not. But on his daughter, yes. No father likes to see his daughter suffer."

"That's out," I said flatly. "You know what our orders are."

"I know what they were. This is my own idea, Marko. Please remember that I am commander here."

I was duty bound to obey him, and I thought that I was going to obey. But as Kresh stepped toward Beth I found myself between them.

"I think that those higher up may have something to say about this," I told Ristal.

"With the information this man can give me I shall be in a position to ignore those higher up," Ristal grinned.

Kresh reached for Beth and I hit him. I knew now what Ristal had in mind. With atomic weapons he could make himself master of Venus, and of Earth. But even more important than that was the thought that he must not harm Beth.

KRESH was coming back at me. I hit him again and he went down. Then the others came piling in. There were four of them, too many for me. I fought like a madman but they overwhelmed me and held me helpless.

"Give him a shot of bental," Ristal ordered. "That ought to quiet him.

Then dump him in a cabin. We'll dispose of him later."

Then Kresh was coming at me with the hypodermic needle. I felt it stab into my arm. He gave me a dose that might have killed an ordinary man.

My senses were leaving me. I knew that I had to overcome the effects of the drug. I knew that I had to get out of that cabin. Somehow I dragged myself out of the bunk and got a porthole open. I crawled through it and dropped to the floor of the barn.

There were some loose boards and I pried them further apart and crawled out into the open. I no longer knew what I was doing; I no longer remembered Beth. I only knew that I had to run and keep on running.

MY BROKEN rib was stabbing into me like a knife. Across my chest the limb of the tree was a dead weight that crushed me. But now I knew who I was and what I was doing.

Despite the agony I managed to get my hands under the limb. I pushed up and felt it move. The pressure on my chest was gone. Inch by inch I slid out from beneath the huge branch. I staggered to my feet.

How much time had elapsed I didn't know. I was running again, but now I was running toward the dark barn. It wouldn't have taken Ristal long to get started. Maybe by now Beth was... I shut the thought from my mind.

I was a few hundred yards away when the first scream came. Through the wind and the pelting rain it came, and it chilled me more than they had done.

My chest was aflame with every panting breath I took. But I ran as I had never run before. I had to get there before she screamed again. I had to stop them from doing this to her.

The barn door was locked. I got my fingers under the edge and ripped the wood away from the lock and went on through and into the ship.

None of them saw me coming. Copperd was tied in a chair, his face contorted and tears streaming down his face. Three of the men held Beth while Ristal and Kresh worked over her. The rest were watching.

They hadn't taken my del gun from me. But I couldn't use it for fear of hitting Beth. I had it out of my pocket and in my hand as I charged across the room.

MY RUSH brought me into point-blank range on a line parallel with Beth's prostrate figure. At the same time her torturers wheeled about to face me, trapped for an instant in the paralysis of complete surprise. Ristal was the first to recover.

"Drop the gun, Marko," he said.

In my weakened condition, habit governed my reflexes. I almost obeyed the order. Then Ristal took a single step forward and I swung the muzzle of the gun upward again.

"You almost had me," I said. "But you are no longer in command. You and Kresh will return as prisoners, to face trial."

I hoped that he would accept the inevitable. Our crew could plead that they had done nothing except follow the orders of their commanding officer. But for Kresh and Ristal there could be no mitigating circumstances.

I hoped that he would accept the inevitable. Our crew could plead that they had done nothing except follow the orders of their commanding officer. But for Kresh and Ristal there could be no mitigating circumstances.

I fired once and there was the smell of searing flesh.

"Kresh?" I asked. He looked down at the faceless figure on the floor and shook his head.

He raised his elbows, leaving his holster exposed. I nodded to one of the crewmen and he stepped forward and removed Kresh's del gun.

"Drop it on the floor," I said. "Then tear off his insignia and lock him in the forward cabin."

It was the end of the mutiny. But I felt no joy at that. My chest pained intolerably, my shoulders sagged in exhaustion. And I had failed in my mission.

Beth was all right. I went to her and tore the electrodes from her wrists and ankles and helped her to her feet. She refused to look at me, even allowing me to untie her father by myself.

"I regret that it turned out this way," I said.

"How could it turn out any other way?" Beth demanded suddenly. "Do you think we'd trust you now?"

Off in the night a siren wailed. I listened while another siren joined the first.

"They're already looking for you," I said. "Which shows how little chance I would have had of getting to you openly. You'd better be going now."

But as I led them to the door I knew I had to make one more attempt.

"Professor Copperd, do you think there might still be hope? We of Venus can offer much to Earth."

"Maybe there is hope," he said, and he looked brighter than I had ever seen him look. "I was reaching the point where I had no faith in the future. But now, knowing that you have solved the problems which we face… Perhaps, if the proper arrangements were made… But you would be risking a great deal to return. And I can assure you that for a long time Venus will be safe. So you have no reason…"

"I have a good reason for coming back," I interrupted. Taking Beth by the shoulders, I swung her about to face me.

"I love you," I said. "I started out to trick you and ended by loving you."

Then her arms were about me and her lips were on mine. I felt my face wet with her tears, and I knew that my love was returned. There were still problems to face, dangers to overcome, but they didn't matter.

"It may be a year," I said. "Perhaps two years."

"I'll be waiting. I'll be standing here, waiting for you."

Now the sirens were very close and there were searchlights sweeping the fields and the woods. I watched Beth and her father walking away and then I closed the door. I should have felt sad, but I didn't. A year or two weren't much. On this planet far from my own, I was leaving my heart, and I would return one day to redeem it.

THE END

Originally Published
Amazing Stories, December, 1948

The HIDDEN WORLD

ISSUE NO. A-10
SUMMER, 1963

Contents

EDITORIAL 1726
    Ray Palmer
MORE ON VOICES IN
    YOUR MIND 1728
    Jim Wentworth
THE CRYSTAL KINGDOM
    OF LIFE 1746
    R.B. Hoag, M.D.
LETTERS 1786
    From The Readers
SEEING IN THE "DARK" .1799
    R.B. Hoag, M.D.

EDITORIAL

By Ray Palmer

THIS IS the tenth book in the HIDDEN WORLD series. In the previous nine issues, the subject of the Shaver Mystery has been thoroughly covered, insofar as the known and previously treated portions are concerned. Also, interspersed, have been various writings which add a bit here and there to the overall picture. In this book we begin the presentation of another kind of writings, the "memory" writings of an Indian who lived in the area of the Grand Canyon some 10,000 years ago, as related by a California doctor who believes he is the reincarnation of this Indian, and writes as the memories come back to him. He has written millions of words, and we can present only about a quarter of a million of his writings. The reader may believe what he wishes about reincarnation, but there is one thing he cannot ignore about the memories of this long-dead Indian, and that is their remarkable confirmatory portions, in respect to all of the writings we have thus far presented, and the book "Oahspe", which, if you haven't read up to now, becomes a necessary portion of the overall evidence we have been trying to present about the Hidden World.

When Shaver first was given Oahspe to read (by your editor) he was violently against it. It is not spirits, he declared. This book is "wool", to cover up the truth - the history given in it is almost precisely true, as I know it, but it must be stripped of its spiritistic character to become credible. The reader of all of these works, can draw his own conclusion, but there is one thing we want to point out, not one of them disagrees as to the essentials, only as to personal interpretation. We have proved that Shaver's picture of the caverns is an "interpretation", his own, based on logic and reason. That is, in regards to its whereabouts and its nature. It is perfectly true that he has "Seen" and "Experienced". No one can prove to him that he was not in the caves. To the spiritualist, who can prove that the spiritualist was not actually traveling in a disembodied state in an astral realm very cavern-like in appearance, and that the things he saw and the voices heard, where not performed by the spirits of the dead? And who can prove to the "madman" that all the things that plagued him to madness were in his own mind, and purely imaginary?

Yet all of these things happen, nobody can disagree. There is only one solution, to agree that they are all things seen as the individual sees them and interprets them, different in interpretation, but identical in source and reality.

Just what is that reality?

To the reader of the twelfth book in this series, and Oahspe, and all the philosophy and mysticism of literature, available in books, the broad picture will be similar, and unarguable. And to each, his own interpretation. None of them will be untrue in essentials. All will be usable in deciding the things that life presents to us for decision. All of them point a road to our destiny that is not up to pure chance, but gives us a choice, and gives us a roadmap that we may not be led into a dead-end road, a trap that could enslave us.

There is much more that we can present. The more unpublished material we have presented, the harder it has become. This book is almost a year late The road to future books seems almost impossibly blocked. We will try. But the events of the past year have horrified us - because they have proven very dangerous and very disastrous. It is only because we know the truth, that we risk further harrassment. And if you think we're kidding, then you have wasted your reading of the first nine books in this series, and we advise you to quit right now! What do you say? Are you with us? - Rap.

1727

MORE ON VOICES IN YOUR MIND

By Jim Wentworth

IF ONE WERE permitted to read the personal mail of Richard S. Shaver, I don't doubt that many letters would contain a sentence like this:

"If, Mr. Shaver, there is truth in your claim of the dero sadistically tormenting surface people, where is the proof?"

Speaking for Shaver, I would like to point out an article I wrote for December, 1960 SEARCH. Here, in Voices In Your Mind, a number of documented accounts were given of people driven to uncharacteristic acts of brutality - and murder! Driven by strange, never-before-experienced "urges". Even that of hearing "voices."

My sources of information were not dusty tomes on neglected top shelves of obscure libraries. Not at all. They came from easily obtainable daily newspapers, magazines, books, etc.

Since writing Voices In Your Mind, I have come across several other accounts (all occurring in 1961) of what is called abnormal human behaviorism, and which to me sounds suspiciously like dero persecution. Before setting them down, let us have a few words on one aspect of the Shaver Mystery.

1728

According to Shaver, "ray operators" are constantly on duty in earth's hidden caverns observing surface people via machines – "telaugs" by name – whose invisible rays penetrate miles of solid rock to capture scenes throughout the globe.

Using the long-enduring machines of the Elder Race, the evil and cannibalistic dero foster surface wars, cause terrible air accidents, train wrecks, etc., and in general bedevil the lives of those above. Bedevil in this manner.

With no effort, the dero could implant sadistic and violent thoughts into a telaug, or telepathic projector. Now augmented thousands of times, the thoughts could be made to penetrate the mind of a surface man, causing this innocent to commit any number of savage crimes like arson, rape, murder....

Sometimes the apprehended person will confess that he tortured, kidnapped, or even killed because of the irresistable bidding of "voices" in his mind. Or that he was responsible for some heinous crime through no fault of his own, his excuse being that God told him to do it.

Were these particular criminals goaded into their actions (consciously or subconsciously) by Shaver's deros? The answer would seem to be a capitalized YES!

Now for those 1961 cases mentioned previously.

Case 1. Irving Waldorf was a 22-year old Reno, Nevada disc-jockey. On February 25, 1961, he arrived in Los Angeles, California. Side streets were then prowled to satisfy "an urge to kill".

Early the next morning he found his victim. When Max Liseki, aged 54, walked past him on an otherwise deserted street, Waldorf sent a bullet into the stranger's back. Four more shots were fired before Waldorf ran to a bus depot where he remained mainly for twenty-four hours. Near midnight, he called detectives and confessed.

He stated that he wanted to kill someone and came to Los Angeles for that purpose as he did not want to perform the act in his home town.

He also said he committed himself for four months of observation in the Nevada State Mental hospital last March

1729

because of fits of depression. Doctors released him with the warning the depression periods would return.

Case 2. By the time Wallace D. Hines reached the age of fifteen, he had acquired a shameful criminal record. Consider: Three car thefts, twenty housebreaks, one stint in reform school.

The reason for his behavior remained a mystery to all concerned - his parents, social workers, juvenile authorities, judges. All tried to straighten his life. All failed. What made him different from others his age?

"Wally" came from a respectable middle class family in a good residential neighborhood. None of his brothers and sisters ever had difficulty with the law. He was not of low intelligence either, for Police Lt. Lionel Clarke said he understood Wally had scored higher than any youth in reform school in intelligence tests.

Still, he did confide to friends that his greatest ambition was "to kill a cop". And on May 11, 1961, he did perform a killing - on himself!

Case 3. He was a wealthy building contractor, Charles Pitelka by name, father of five, and resident of nearby Lockport, in Mill County, Illinois. His children ranged in age from ten years to ten months.

On May 14, 1961, he murdered them all, including his 33-year old wife, Vivian, and ended his own life by gas.

Authorities believed it to be a murder-suicide case, indicated by Charles' note who, at one point, wrote: "I'm the devil . . . my brother, Frank, knows all about me."

Case 4. A.O. Smith Corporation, a suburban manufacturing firm of Houston, Texas, employed Charles E. White as a machine operator. This 36-year old, 200 pounder of six feet one inch was described as a "nice guy" and "friendly as a kitten, but he could roughhouse it with the best of them."

On the afternoon of May 17, 1961, he stopped work, began quoting the scriptures, and sang hymns like "What a Friend We Have in Jesus".

Taken by his fellow workers to the plant doctor, the latter called White's wife and family physician. He was then brought to Methodist Hospital which is ranked as one of the best in treatment and research in the U.S.

Here White went berserk. He stabbed six persons, two fatally. His victims were hospital personnel and a 54-year old bedridden patient.

With an eleven inch knife, he ran down hallways, into a surgical ward, etc., quoting scriptures.

"Such is the sin of life," he sang.

Blood-soaked, White was subdued only after the police had used tear gas, six pistols, and a shotgun blast that all but tore his arm off. Each time they shot him, he looked at them and muttered: "Ashes to ashes and dust to dust."

Commented one of the police officers, H.D. Gilbert:

When we arrived, they told us this person had already killed two people and was cornered in a room. He was standing at the foot of the bed with a large bloody knife in his right hand and a water pitcher in the left.

"He kept quoting scripture. He would ask us to leave, and walk around the room slashing at curtains, the window, and the bed. We talked to him for about 12 to 15 minutes, then decided to call for help."

Case 5. Just as was done in Voices In Your Mind, I will again discuss a Billy Graham MY ANSWER column of September 1, 1961, where the following question was asked:

"Do you believe that there are demons (the kind Jesus cast out) in the world today? If so, how do you recognize them?"

The American evangelist agreed to this idea, then quoted an unknown who once said that if the devil was dead, he left a lot of orphans behind. But the truth is that Satan is just as active as he was in the days of Christ. Demons are his "agents" in this world, which is his domain.

As for how to recognize them, Billy Graham wrote that when a person is drawn into irrational, uncontrollable evil, he may be regarded as demon-possessed. Heinous crimes are often committed by people who claim, "I don't know why I did it. I just couldn't help myself!"

Asking why men are drawn into lust, greed, hatred and all kinds of evil, he replied that he believes demonic power often motivates them, and ended with the words:

"The Scriptures attribute much of the evil in the world to the activity of demons."

To which I, the writer of this article, cannot resist adding that Shaver undoubtedly would remark: "Demons or dero - same thing, really."

Case 6. In the Canadian city of Hamilton, Ontario, two boys tossed a flaming torch through the bathroom window of a house. Andy Carvatos, owner of the house, who also witnessed the unwarranted act, saw the boys run away. This was on November 18, 1961.

As Carvatos fought the flames with a blanket, his wife led their children - aged four, five, six and seven - to safety. He told investigators he had no enemies. The destruction seemed senseless. Why this uncalled-for behavior on the part of the boys?

The above half dozen cases may, or may not, have involved deros. Having no inside information, I cannot be positive either way. I do, however, believe in the possibility of the dero motivating the uncharacteristic actions of Irving Waldorf, Wallace D. Hines, etc.

Jimmy DeBruin, aged twenty, worked on a plantation near Farm Datoen, South Africa, where he lived.

On August 10, 1960, there occurred here what appeared to be poltergeist activity consisting of tossed bottles, moving furniture, etc. When things got too violent, the police were called.

Accompanied by three constables, Police Chief John Wessels reported that when he walked through the house and left the lounge, an ornamental sealed-glass bowl with a flower fell from a shelf to shatter four feet away.

Suddenly, as there came a painful scream from DeBruin, all eyes swung upon him - and stared in fascinated horror.

On the youth's bare legs (he was wearing shorts) appeared inexplicable cuts! Blood streamed forth.

The next day, two closely watching detectives witnessed a deep gash materialize on his chest which was covered by a white shirt. This was inflicted by - what unseen agency?

The terrifying attacks did not abate, but continued for several days. Mostly, the slashes were cleanly cut, as though made with a razor blade or surgical instruments.

That the boy had indulged in self-infliction was never for a moment considered by the police. Finally the phenomena stopped.

In discussing the above case in his book, STRANGEST OF ALL, Frank Edwards regarded the whole affair as nothing more than poltergeist activity.

Poltergeist activity? I echo.

Or dero activity? queries Shaver.

In his other book, STRANGER THAN SCIENCE, Frank Edwards tells about a weird happening in Manila on May 10, 1951.

Eighteen year old Clarita Villaneuva was a homeless, drifting victim of the war. She was arrested when, in the centre of a small crowd on a street corner, she screamed that she was being attacked and bitten.

Most of the low-class onlookers cheered her on, winked knowingly in their belief that she was insane. Dope addict, maybe, or absinthe? Could it be an epileptic seizure?

Once the struggling girl was locked in the police cell, she fell sobbing to the floor.

She claimed the Thing had bitten her, leaving eight sets of teeth marks. Her pleas for the police to see for themselves were ignored. The man-like Thing (as described by Clarita) had big, bulging eyes, wore a loose black cape, and seemed to float in the air when he desired.

Again came the screams, the shrieks that the Thing was approaching through the bars.

Unlocking the cell door, a policeman led the screaming girl into the hall where he saw teeth marks appear on her upper arms and shoulders - livid marks surrounded by what seemed to be saliva.

An examination of Clarita's marks were made by the Medical Examiner, Dr. Mariana Lara, Mayor Lacson, and the Chief of Police. That it was self-inflicted was out of the question, for who could bite oneself on the back of the neck or shoulders?

1733

Next morning, as she was about to be taken into court to face vagrancy charges, Clarita screamed that she was being bitten by the returned Thing! Present were several reporters and Dr. Lara.

Held by two strong policemen, all witnessed teeth marks sinking deep into her arms, the palms of her hands, and her neck. For five minutes the attack continued until, mercifully, she sank to the floor in a dead faint.

Dr. Lara's examination convinced him that this was not an epileptic seizure. The bites were real enough, and not self-inflicted. Mayor Lacson was called. Also the Archbishop.

Upon the former's arrival thrity minutes later, Clarita had regained consciousness. Her arm-bites were badly swollen, and bruises covered the palm of one thickened hand where teeth prints had been deeply imbedded.

Again, as Mayor Lacson and Dr. Lara accompanied her to the prison hospital, Clarita began shrieking. The Thing was back, and joined by a helper, another big-eyed creature!

Livid teeth marks (as later testified by the Mayor) appeared on each side of her throat and on her index finger. Even while he held her hand, watching, one set of teeth prints was deeply indented.

Not once during the fifteen minute car ride to the prison hospital did the attacks cease. Then they did just that, and Clarity began her slow recovery, never to have such a horrible experience return.

Well, what can I say about the true case just recounted? Only this. That the underground inhabitants have access to machines capable of producing all of the phenomena in which Clarita Villaneuva was involved.

Note, please, that it is machines - manufactured machines - causing the weird happenings and not anything that smacks of the supernatural.

During March, 1962, newspapers carried a letter in Ann Landers' popular syndicated column. It went:

"Dear Ann Landers: I'm a senior in high school (female) and am considered above average in intelligence. I get along well in my studies and I'm sure people think I am

1734

normal. But I have a feeling that there is something wrong with me - upstairs, I mean.

"For the past few months I've been petrified of taking even a short automobile trip with my father. He's a good driver and has never been in an accident. I have no real reason to worry. Yet, whenever I say goodby to my friends, I always have the weird feeling I will never see them again.

"Also, when I go to wake up my sister in the morning I am afraid she is dead. These morbid thoughts have me scared stiff. Do you think I am going crazy? - PETRIFIED."

Replied Ann:

"Dear Petrified: Everyone has fears and flashes of morbid thoughts now and then. They are not signs of insanity. If you are having these thoughts every day, however, I suggest you see a psychiatrist and get to the bottom of what is bothering you."

Ann Landers' answer was the expected one - "see a psychiatrist." How startled her readers would have been had she remarked: "Could be that you have come to the attention of the mad dero as described by Richard Shaver, and they are getting their 'kicks' by tormenting you with the telaug machines of the Ancients."

I do not claim with bursting confidence that this is so. I say only that the dero could be responsible.

Residing in Amherst village, Nova Scotia, eighteen year old Esther Cox lived with her married sister, Olive, and her brother-in-law, Daniel Teed. Other occupants of the small frame house on Princess Street near Church were another sister, Jane, and a brother of Daniel, John.

It all began with a dream Esther experienced early one August night in 1879. Here Esther saw the facial transformation of her family from normalcy to the growling countenances of bears. The terrible, unprecedented nightmare invloving a herd of charging black bulls, continued.

Esther was a nervous, moody, insecure person. One evening a suiter, Bob McNeil, took her for a horse and buggy ride. A full moon shone, and things were serene until a tremor shook the young man from head to foot.

1735

Jumping to the ground, face contorted, he whipped out a revolver which he leveled at his cowering companion. There came, at that moment, the sounds of a fast-approaching carriage, whereupon Bob leaped back up beside Esther. Given the whip, the horse charged back into the village.

Esther was let off, unharmed, in front of her house. Bob rode away, never to be seen again.

On the fifth night of her terrifying experience, Esther told her bed-mate sister, Jane, that she felt a mouse under the blankets. A thorough search revealed nothing.

With that, a hatbox rose off the dresser. Drifting across the room, it settled on a chair, much to the amazement of the two girls.

Five more nights passed. At ten o'clock, Esther complained to Jane of feeling ill when, suddenly, her hair stood on end. She leaped from the bed, shrieking loudly that she was flying apart.

The outburst brought Olive into the room, fast, as Esther fell back on the bed. Now her sisters saw a horrifying sight, that of Esther's body swelling to an enormous size, accompanied by moans of pain.

When the aroused Daniel and John Teed burst into the room, there came a thunderous report. Lightning? No, not from a clear and starry sky.

Esther's body was hideously distorted. After three more loud reports, her body slowly returned to normal size. An exhausted sleep enfolded her. Incredibly, she awoke the next morning feeling like her old self.

Again, five days slipped by. At ten p.m. Esther's bedroom shook with a series of cannon-like explosions. She started to swell. This time with greater speed and violence. Shrieks of torment came from the bloated caricature of a human being.

Suddenly the sheets and blankets from the bed tore free and shot off to a corner of the room, squirming and twisting as if alive as the sisters retrieved them. To keep the bedclothes in position, the family was forced to sit on them around the edge of the bed.

1736

While doing so, Esther's pillow slid from under her head. Pressing itself into the trembling face of John Teed, it then resumed its former place.

The next morning, Daniel Teed took off a few hours from his job as foreman of the Amherst Shoe Factory. He called on the famous Dr. Caritte with his incredible story. Undismayed by the expected scepticism, Daniel was glad of the other's promise to pay him a house visit that very evening and examine Esther.

When, after ten o'clock, the doctor arrived, Esther was in seizure. In entering her bedroom, a piece of wall plaster fell at his feet. It was placed on a chair. The patient was then examined in an unaccountably noisy room. Came a rythmic pounding of furniture, jumping violently. Loud, now-familiar reports were heard.

Again Esther's pillow swooped about the room. John Teed went after it, grabbed it, and in utter amazement discovered he was powerless to secure it. Once more the pillow slid under Esther's head.

Baffled, Dr. Caritte remained with Esther for several hours until the phenomena ended with the usual three reports. Quickly regaining normalcy, the patient fell into a deep sleep.

The doctor's parting advice to the others was to watch Esther closely, for to leave her alone would be dangerous.

Dr. Caritte returned the following night before ten to give Esther a morphia injection in hopes that the strong opiate would calm the nightly disturbances.

No luck. For, at the hour of ten, there came a burst of sardonic laughter. Esther fell to the floor, screaming. From the roof was heard a pounding noise which drew curious townspeople.

With the family's assistance, Dr. Caritte was holding Esther on her bed when all heard a scratching sound. It came from the wall where, inexplicably, large letters wrote:

"Esther Cox, you are mine to kill!"

Who - or what - was causing these amazing things to happen? Was it the vanished suitor, Bob McNeil, as Jane

Cox suggested the next morning? At this, three affirmative knocks sounded on the table before her.

Spiritual personalities - six in number - admitted that they had created all the phenomena that had plagued Esther for five months.

In December of 1879, Esther was bedded for two weeks with diphtheria. Two more weeks found her convalescing in Sackville, New Brunswick, at the home of another sister, Mrs. John Snowden.

Afterwards, she returned to the Teed home. A few days passed peacefully. The whole family sat in the parlor, along with a guest, the Reverend Dr. Clay, pastor of the local Baptist Church.

Suddenly Esther jumped erect. Fearfully, she pointed to a corner of the room.

"Look there!" she screamed. "Look there! Don't you see him! He says I must leave the house tonight. If I don't - he will set a fire in the loft under the roof. What shall I do! Merciful God, who will take me! I wish I were dead!"

She collapsed, sobbing, while the others stared at the corner indicated, and saw nothing. Nothing except for a dozen lighted matches which materialized and fell about the room.

If the Teed house was ignited, the strong wind blowing from the west could turn Amherst village into a holocaust. The fire marshalls dared not take the risk. Esther was therefore removed to the home of kindly, sympathetic Mr. and Mrs. John White, and their daughter, Mary.

Here the disturbances continued. There came the sound of heavy footsteps at all hours. Obscenities from unseen sources were shouted. Several of the many fires that started mysteriously were almost uncontrollable.

Visitors of the White's were mercilessly mocked, ridiculed and insulted by voices of the invisibles.

Esther was given a job in the White's restaurant until, after a spell, she returned home.

Early in March, 1880, she was examined by a committee of prominent scientists in St. John, New Brunswick. Their report stated the impossibility of fraud.

Next to enter the scene was Walter Hubbel, journalist from the same city. When he went to Amherst to spend six weeks in the Teed household, he was then admittedly skeptical of the things said to be happening to Esther Cox. That he intended to expose the girl in her "rigged-up" house as a fraudulent medium, was undoubted.

But his skepticism changed, drastically, when he saw with his own eyes, and heard with his own ears, the strange goings-on.

An umbrella, plucked from his hand, was thrown over his head. His shoulder was grazed by a carving knife that darted out of the deserted kitchen. A large, empty chair moved about friskily, charged at Hubbel sitting in a chair, collided violently, and sent him sprawling. Voices sounded insultingly. Matches materialized out of thin air. Trumpet sounds assailed his ears, lasting all day. The date was June 28, 1880. Later the trumpet itself fell into the parlor. Soiled to the touch, it was found to be made of a metal similar to German silver, and was presented to Hubbel.

Having reached the point where she could no longer remain with her near-hysterical family, Esther left to take up residence with friends at the Van Amburghs' farm some distance from Amherst.

Thus did the phenomena cease.

When, on August 1, 1880, Walter Hubbel visited her, he found a contented Esther Cox finally at peace in her new surroundings.

And so ends the Esther Cox story as taken from J. Lewis Toole's January, 1952 FATE article, The Possession of Esther Cox.

Before leaving my detailed account of it, let us go over it again, quickly, but this time with one big difference. The difference being that the Shaver Mystery will be strongly in mind.

What was the event that initially changed Esther's normal life to the approximately ten month old nightmare it became? It was a dream, a dream of nightmarish proportions, and one that Shaver's deros could produce with laughable ease via underground mech. Such dero-operated machines could

1739

explain all of the phenomena associated with Esther.

Like: Bob McNeil's unaccountable behavior with intent to kill - Esther's false conviction that a mouse was under her blankets - a hatbox rising off the dresser and moving about the room - the feeling, or delusion, of "flying apart" - Esther's painfully swelling body - thunderous reports - bed sheets, blankets and pillows tearing free to head for a corner of the room. And . . . -falling wall plaster, noise, jumping furniture, sardonic laughter, writing on the wall, the admittance that spiritual personalities were responsible for all weird events.

Another claim of Esther's was that of seeing, and hearing, some male creature making threatening remarks in a room's corner. Remarks such as, if Esther did not leave the house that night, the loft under the roof would be set ablaze. The creature was invisible to all other members of the Teed family then present.

However, something else was seen by all - the materialization of a dozen lighted matches falling about the room. This inexplicable happening in the presence of Esther Cox reminded me at once of other incendiary phenomena in the BOOKS OF CHARLES FORT.

It happened in December, 1889, with the starting of a fire in a mahogany desk in the centre of the Secretary of War's office in Washington, D.C. Several official papers that were later claimed of no special value and irreplaceable, were destroyed. Undiscovered by Secretary Proctor was the fire's origin. As a non-smoker, matches were never kept about his desk.

During the night of April 20, 1920, there occurred in the War Office in Constantinople (where are stored the archieves) a fire of unknown origin. Here, beyond a locked iron door inaccessible to entry until the afternoon, many important documents were destroyed.

In September of that same year, 1920, there was the simultaneous breaking out of three fires in different departments of the Government Office, in Tothill Street, Westminster, London.

What we have here, it would seem, are government

papers whose importance, admitted or denied, were done away with by fire of mysterious origin. If a human agency was responsible, was it the underground inhabitants of whom Shaver talks? And was it because they knew those papers would reveal the long-kept secret of their existence and, in order to insure their safety, Elder mech was used to destroy the papers?

The cavern people, then, operate machines capable of destroying vital papers by fire no matter how heavily protected they are.

Going along with this line of reasoning, I ask still another question, this one regarding Esther Cox.

Were the matches that materialized out of thin air in her presence caused by, not the spirit world, but by the quite material, hidden world as described by Richard Shaver?

And, finally, does his Mystery explain the whole affair of the unfortunate Canadian from Amherst, Nova Scotia?

The girl was a mere child. Only ten years old. Her name was Grace Budd, and on June 3, 1928, she was strangled in an old abandoned bungalow on the outskirts of Greenburgh, in Westchester County, near New York City.

"When she was dead" - I am quoting from Alan Bentham's book SEX CRIMES AND SEX CRIMINALS - "he (the killer) stripped off her clothes and chopped off her head with the cleaver. He sawed the body through above the navel, separated it into three parts. He wrapped the head in old newspapers and hid it in the cottage outhouse. Then he carefully wrapped other parts of the body in a cloth and took them home with him.

"During the next nine days he cooked them up in various ways with onions, carrots and strips of bacon. Then he feasted on them. Throughout this period, according to his signed confession, he was in a constant state of sexual excitement. Later he returned to the cottage and wrapped the girl's bones in brown paper and threw them behind a stone wall."

Who was this degenerate of many aliases who did such a monstrous thing? What was his background?

He was short, kindly-looking Albert Howard Fish, born

1741

in 1870 in Washington, D.C., and the abducted Grace was not his sole victim. When captured six and a half years after her murder, detctives uncovered evidence that Fish had slain - and devoured - eight children, with the possible correct total being as high as fifteen!

It turned out that he had a police record of eight arrests, having served several short jail terms from grand larceny to sending obscene letters through the mail. This latter act of his was done at regular intervals to the bereaved Budd family until, through it, Fish gave himself away and was finally caught.

In addition to his practising cannibalism, he openly admitted he enjoyed drinking human blood. He was described by examining psychiatrists as being the most abnormal individual they had ever encountered, or read about. The police called him "the most perverted and depraved fiend in the annals of crime."

Surprisingly enough, he was intensely religious, this sex maniac who never drank or smoked, and spent much of his time in jail reading the Bible.

Fish married a nineteen year old girl when he was twenty-eight. Six children came of this union. After some twenty years of marriage, his wife ran off with a boarder from their house when their youngest was three years old. Fish supported his brood as a painter, decorator, and odd job man until they all reached adulthood. He had five grandchildren.

When approximately fifty-five, he developed "an acute religious psychosis", experiencing all kinds of hallucinations and delusions. Not only did visions of Christ and the angels appear, but supernatural voices were also heard.

Once he was found by his children atop a hill, hands raised heavenward, shouting:

"I am the Christ!"

He told psychiatrists that God commanded him to castrate young boys, and to offer up human sacrifice.

That his immediate family possessed a strong taint of psychosis is proved when we learn the following facts:

(1) A paternal uncle died in a Maine mental institution.

1742

(2) A paternal aunt was said to be "completely crazy". (3) Fish's mother was considered "queer", for she often "heard voices" and "had visions". (4) A half-brother (by his father's first marriage) died in a California mental hospital. (5) A younger, feeble-minded brother died of hydrocephalus (dropsy of the brain). (6) Another brother was a chronic alcoholic. (7) A sister suffered some sort of "mental affliction".

One noteable contrast was a distant relative, Hamilton Fish, who was U.S. Secretary of State under President Grant.

At the trial of Albert Fish, the jury pronounced him guilty. So this warp-minded man died in the electric chair, coolly, calmly, and with obvious enjoyment.

What drove him to commit his sadistic deeds? How explain the tremendous strength of his compulsions?

If the Shaver Mystery enters the picture and the answer lies in dero persecution, then it is the dero who are fully responsible for the many vile murders committed by the unfortunate puppet who was helplessly under their control.

When the dero want some "fun", they usually go after a person - a single individual - from the surface world. Thus begins unrelenting heckling, needling, tormenting, often ending with the innocent's laughed-at death.

In Fish's case, it would seem that for many years the dero gave their attention to his whole family, including aunts and uncles. Certainly they have the wonder machines to produce all the phenomena of hallucinations, delusions, voices, etc. just described.

It is claimed that the dero do not always go to the extreme of inducing an upper-worlder to kill. There are times when they seem to be satisfied to merely torment.

Examples of this sort of bedevilment could be the "Hard Luck Hanna", that certain type of person who attracts bad luck with such persistent regularity that one can only gasp in amazement.

Misfortunes are experienced, like a broken leg one week, cuts from shattered glass the next, followed by a bumped head against an open cupboard, a fall in the bathtub, tripping down the cellar steps, a stove burn. And so on and on, month after month. Maybe year after year.

To see them with an arm or a leg in a cast, or hobbling along on crutches, or bedded with a bandaged head from a concussion, is a common sight. Very natural for this kind of individual who psychiatrists say are "accident prone", that subconsciously they desire to hurt themselves, enjoying the extra sympathy and attention thereby acquired. The pain they suffer assuages the guilt for "sins" that are real or imagined.

So, in a very real sense, they purposefully have accidents despite sharp pains and expensive medical bills. But to convince them of this would indeed be a difficult task.

Well, maybe so. Maybe this explanation from the psychiatrists is the correct one. But if all things are possible, then it follows that the psychiatrists could be incorrect, and Richard Shaver could have the one and only true answer.

Dero persecution.

By a sort of odd coincidence, while putting the finishing touches to this article, I came across an old newspaper clipping tucked inside a long-forgotten 1948 diary. So unusual is this item, and so appropriate to this article, that I thought it fitting to end More On Voices In Your Mind with its inclusion.

On Friday, July 16, 1948, three children were crossing a sixty foot high viaduct in Cincinnati, Ohio. They were Edna Kidwell, aged eleven, Patricia Jackson, aged eight, and (presumably) her three year old brother, Charles.

Then, quite unexpectedly, tragedy struck in the form of gaunt, huge-handed, six-foot-four Harry Robertson who was approaching the trio.

Patricia had fallen behind when she stopped to buckle her shoe. She had told the others to keep on going, that she would catch up with them.

The itinerate grabbed Patricia and threw her over the rail of the viaduct. The girl's screams had her two playmates swinging around. Harry headed for them.

Witnesses to the unprovoked attack were John Theobald and Walter Backherns. On their motorcycles, they had seen the whole nightmare about fifty feet away. Harry's wild look was one Theobald would never forget. He and his chum yelled to the two children to run, which caused Harry to turn to them. Minutes later he was captured.

Why did this man hurl Patricia to her death? What brought on this senseless violence, this casual destruction of a human life? But, first, who was he?

He was a thirty-three year old war veteran who had served a three year jail sentence in Virginia for housebreaking. He was, also, a former patient of a veteran's mental hospital.

At police headquarters he confessed that he hears "voices" that call him "yellow", and that "radioactivity" was responsible for his actions. This latter statement was beyond his ability to explain.

THE CRYSTAL KINGDOM OF LIFE

By R. B. Hoag, M. D.

*I*T IS TOO much taken for granted that what the geologists have said in their books is so. We need to do thinking ourselves about all the important matters of science. It is not so that great glacial-epochs were, in eras of the past. It is not so that the earth was once a great mass of molten rock. It is not so that the great geologic records of the earth would have had to be covered very deep with ice for many thousands of years. It would be too much to go into all that in a book of this kind. Great masses of land float in very heavy water as iron floats in mercury many hundreds of miles down in the one great ocean that Earth is. In ancient times no sea-bottoms were, between the great masses of land, so that then, in those ancient eras, the continents and islands could move. Even now, though the great ocean is with a sea-bottom covering it everywhere, some movement of continents is possible.

It is not good to believe that everything has been all worked out already. It is good to get so you know that great nature is a person (not merely some set of natural-laws that human persons have thought was all there is to nature).

It is not good to think that the work in any science is about all done so that no longer is there any interesting thinking to do.

In the sea there is a tiny kind of shell called Globigerina. It is the shell of a tiny shellfish. Each one of the myriads of tiny shells that go down to the bottom of the sea after the tiny shellfish dies, is still a living thing; the shell is still alive. How interested I was, years ago, when I read in a big book of geology I have, that what is known as green sand forms in place in the tiny empty shells of the Globigerinas. The geologists call green sand "glauconite". That name is a misleading one for it means merely the material of green sand when it is in the amorphous state. I was much interested to read that green sand forms in place in the tiny shells down in the sea. How is that? Are there not plenty of other places in which those green silicates can crystalize out of the sea water? Why do the chemicals that have to get together to form that complex silicate choose those tiny shells to get together in? The complex silicate seems to need something to get it started to crystallizing out of the sea water. Those crystals grow there and may fill the little shell. The shell itself may disappear. The silicate may go on growing there, so that the crystal of green sand is a larger one than is usual. Much of that crystallization of that particular kind of complex silicate may be formed, for there are formations called "green sand marl". We are led to suppose that the cause of that crystallization of the complex silicate in those many tiny shells is some remaining organic matter in those tiny shells.

You read that statement and go on. You are not a scientist, so you take what the person says in that book of science, and pass on to the next thing he tells about. I myself did that way for years. Then I came to see from very many things that my mind had been brooding over, that there is, actually, a kingdom of life below the plant-kingdom of life. How much that has helped me to understand the very many complex things that you have to understand, if you are to know anything deep about human life.

1747

I was many years getting to the place where I saw that there are very many examples of what goes on when your own teeth grow. That is an example of what living crystals do. The growing of calcareous shells about shellfish is the same kind of a process that the growing of teeth is, in your own case. You know, probably, that there is what is known as the "enamel organ" from which your teeth grow up. I am sure that in the so-called enamel-organ there are living crystals of some compound of calcium. In the ends of the bones of the young human person there are osteoblasts. I believe that in those protoplasmic cells living crystals of some compound of calcium are. How much calcium and silicon are used by animals and plants. Without those stiffening substances no evolution of higher forms of animals would have been possible. I believe that ordinary wood is a kind of crystallized carbon-compound. (You need to deepen your idea of what crystals are, of course, if you are to think much, deep into the great problems of life.) I believe that in the protoplasm of all living cells, both that of plants, and that of animals, there are myriads of living tiny crystals of different kinds. I know that you may smile as you read this, you who do not realize how many years I have been thinking about the interesting things of biology. Of course those crystals would grow, grow so big that there would be no room for any protoplasm in the cell - if nature had not, long since, solved that one of the many problems. If the living of the crystal was to continue on indefinitely, then as one part grew, another part would have to be dissolved away; for only while the crystal grows does it live.

Very long ago a good partnership was formed between protoplasm and living crystals: "You protect me from external injuries" said the protoplasm, "and I will keep you continuously supplied with what you need for your kind of life and I will continuously remove the 'dead matter' that you are through with: that waste matter is just what I need for my living". No good understanding of the processes of living can be got, unless you go deeper than the scientists of these times go. They are going around in circles,

1748

as the saying is. We need to call a halt to their continuing searching after new things, smashing atoms - as if to say: "We have made all the important discoveries there are to make in the molecular-world, so now we must descend into the atomic world". Life is the deep explanation of most of the phenomena of nature. How can we get so we can understand the things nature does, unless we first get so we know who great invisible nature is?

That tiny Globigerina-person died, the protoplasmic member of that co-partnership. How was the crystal-person, who was left alive, to do, now that his good friend had died? The tiny shell went down in the sea water. It came to rest on the bottom there. It was soon in need of more calcium carbonate. Well, there was plenty of that in solution in the water. "I see," thought the tiny living shell to himself, "I can still get plenty of calcium carbonate for my living and for the work I do. What is this? What I feel is not just the same as what I used to feel, when my partner was having his soft body right up next to my growing living part of me. I believe I like this new experience. Now I have calcium to work with and I have silicon. I'll see how it will be to use this new stuff; I like a change from what I have been having all my life." So, a complete iron-containing green silicate grew there within the tiny shell.

In the hot-springs that are active in various parts of the earth much calcium or silicon is used. That is not just crystallized out of the hot water as the deposit in the old-fashioned teakettle was crystallized out, by evaporating of much water in which was a little calcium carbonate. Tiny living beings do that work. In the case of the lime-secreting algae, the calcium bicarbonate is removed from the water. That throws down crystals of calcium carbonate. (The presence of calcium bicarbonate in the water makes for the easy solution of calcium carbonate. Take out of that water the bicarbonate of calcium and the calcium carbonate that use silicon, some chemical process not yet understood causes the silicon to crystallize out, as some kind of silica, into the crystals of which some water enters into chemical combination. (Opal is an example of this hydrous crystalline silica.)

How very much limestone there is in the formations of the rocks of the earth. That is not made from powdered shells. There may be many shells in some limestones, but most of the limestones and dolomites are fine-grained rocks. I believe that those very extensive formations are the geologic records of work done by myriads of living crystals in eras of the past, even in the era before any plants had been evolved in the earth.

Tiny living crystals, very far back in the history of life, were the only living beings in the earth. What first begins a growth is ever in that as its innermost about which all is organized. Living crystals of different kinds, myriads of tiny ones, are what makes living possible from plant and animal protoplasm. How could the protoplasm do its work if no small chemists were there to do that absolutely necessary work of getting the needed special substances separated out from the solutions that were in the protoplasm? Tiny living crystals do all the chemical work of plants and of animals.

I am no laboratory-worker with the best microscopes and the best techniques of dissecting down into very small living protoplasmic cells. For many years very many good industrious patient scientists have done that kind of work. Of course some of that kind of work was necessary. How well we, who cannot ourselves do that laboratory work, can avail ourselves of what the thousands of that kind of workers have worked out. We need something much more important than that kind of work. The laboratories could close down for fifty years - and the people of the human race would be very much better off - for many thinkers would set to make use of what had been already worked out in the many fine laboratories. In one of the laboratories in Canada, years ago, a deep thinker put several discoveries together - and good very useful insulin was the result. How would it have been for the human race if that scientist had merely kept on with his ordinary laboratory work? It is the use of the deeper purer mind that is needed by the anguished human race. We are all down in an age-old HELL! No mere use of

1750

millions of ordinary minds (reasoning minds) will ever get us up out of that. There is urgent need for many persons to turn to deep thinking.

One time, very long ago, there were no solids at all, only gases and liquids. "How could that be?" you, the reader of this book, may ask. "If there were no solids, where would gases and liquids come from?" Gases came before liquids, in the great world. Liquids are the result of a very interesting thing; a change has to take place in the atoms of that substance. I will tell you what I believe is a very important scientific fact. I was thinking, not many days ago, yet again about great Sun (our Star). I knew that stars are not hot. Of course they could not be anything but very very very cold - at absolute-zero temperature, or below that. (How could black sun-spots be in Sun if the temperature there was anything near what the scientists seem to believe it is? All things there would be incandescent, would they not? How could anything black be there?) The principles that enabled some scientists to work out the idea, absolute-zero temperature, makes you know, when you think long and deeply into it, that Sun, and all the other stars are at, or below, that degree of temperature. I knew that the stars are all very cold. (Of course I know about how the astronomers are saying that they can, with their very wonderful instruments, know the state of matter of the great heavenly-bodies. I know what I know about the wonderful findings of some of the prominent astronomers. One brilliant idea is that we are living in an expanding universe, in which all the heavenly bodies are traveling away from us with the speed of light. I will say no more about the astronomers now.)

What is the ether? I believe that the stars are all great safe storage places for very much liquid ether. I believe that liquid ether is the most dangerous, most powerful explosure there is. It has to be kept safe. Far from any planet, compressed by a tremendous "atmospheric pressure", at or below absolute-zero temperature, it is safe. That, I believe the invisible person, nature, worked all out very long ago, long before there were any planets in the world.

1751

Go out of your house, if the time is right for that, and look up to our star. Do that. You yourself have some good astronomical instruments. Put them to good use; you will not injure your eyes if you look steadily up into the blaze of him. Do not go get a smoked glass; look with your unprotected eyes at sun. Practise that thing. In a few weeks you can get so you can know for yourself that what I say is true. You will see the liquid ether of sun yourself. Blue. Sun, and all the other stars are a beautiful satisfying cool radiant blue. You should take notice (when you get so you can see the satisfying blue of sun), that that cool deep blue is a smaller globe than is the great yellow blaze that at first your eyes see. You get so you can look away the Corona-phenomena so as to see the actual cool satisfying sun himself. You even see through the very porous frozen ether that crusts over all the whole titanic globular fluid mass of the liquid ether. You may see for yourself that blue is the real primary color. (How much more blue there is in the spectrum than there is of any other of the colors.)

(Editor's Note: Apparently this is in direct contradiction of the experiences in 1963 during the solar eclipse, in which authorities warned against looking at the sun, because of the danger of serious eye injury, and in which numerous persons were reported to have actually suffered such injury. Therefore, the editor of this magazine wishes to point this fact out to you, and to caution you not to risk damage no matter what this account says. It is true, however, that your editor has personally met people who made a practice of staring at the sun, and who did report that it turned blue, and whose sight was apparently perfect and unharmed. It would be interesting to have reports from persons who have looked long at the sun without injury, but it would not be a good thing to experiment without many such accounts to refute the opinion of the medical profession that staring at the sun will cause eye injury. It is a matter that must be settled by positive previous evidence. But do NOT experiment carelessly in a matter like this. We will report any evidence we receive. We invite positive proof either way. If you know anything about this, please write to this magazine.

1752

The reader will understand the reason for this footnote. It is because if you do look at the sun, and are injured, you will say it was because this book said it was not harmful, and that we are therefore responsible, and you will sue us. This is an unfortunate part of our law, that one can thrust responsibility onto another. Therefore, we must protect ourselves. We say, do not look at the sun - it will harm you to do so (listen to the authorities, instead). It may not be so, but we don't KNOW that it is. Thus, be warned - you look at your own risk!)

Be in deep thought often as you read these things that I am telling you. These things came not from out any laboratory experiments with expensive instruments; they came as the result of very much terrible anguish suffered for many hard years; it took different kinds of psychologic pressures on one to get me to think these things out. I am one of the ordinary common people. I am one who wants no notoriety at all. All I want is that these practical-useful scientific facts may be got out into public view, so that those who care to may begin to make use of some of them for themselves.

In this book I will have to be very careful, watch my step all the time - maybe some of the very well-read specialists will be like sharp-eyed eagles, looking - till I make some mistake - so that they can swoop down, grip that up, and show it to all people everywhere. I am not very wise in the matters of mere information. I am trying to make good use of the few good scientific books that I am able to get to look into. I have, yet again, gone carefully through a three-volume well-known Geology, so as to freshen up for this work that I must do. Also, I got from the library a number of recent books. I know now what the scientists still believe, regarding the origin of this planet we live on. I have to be as careful as I can be to do full justness to the good work many good scientists have done in the field of science that Geology is. I will probably make mistakes. Take what I offer to you for what it may be worth to you. All atoms of whatever kind are, I believe, like our Sun is in a kind of a way.

1753

Sun has as its active region, a thick shell all around, known as the Corona. Within that shell is a region in which there is not much "self-activity". Outside of that Corona much more "self-activity" is possible. The corona is far out in space from the central nucleus of the great solar-system. You need to see with the eyes of your mind, this titanic protoplasmic-cell. It has a kind of a nucleus to it, the great globe of liquid ether closed in with what you might call a nuclear-membrane, made up of living crystals of ether that could form only at that very low temperature a frozen crust. No gas of any kind can be there, and no liquid (there in the crust). Below the crust is clear transparent liquid ether. (The liquid ether itself is not blue. It gives off a cool radiant blue light. It, that blue light, is what you see when you look up into the sky, everywhere). Clear liquid ether is the source of the ordinary ether we here in our planet know something about; (ether is the "source" through which all our substances and powers come to us). It is like a gas. I have to be not merely general in what I say about these deep matters; so be very patient with me. If my book goes out to many people, it may be that some good deep-thinking scientists will look into my theory for themselves. I who write these things am only one poor common person. My education was not more than millions of other persons have had. By much deep thinking during many years, I got so I was using my deep mind. I have had to live through many years of terrible anguish. I am very deeply concerned about the bad HELL the whole human race is down in. I have known for many years that the practise of breaches of nature's necessary laws is what got the human race down into HELL, and what keeps us all down in it. That has been on my mind and heart for very many years. If the people knew how things are in the great world, they would not be nearly so careless about the doing of many things they now do. I am myself learning that even small breaches of nature's necessary laws cause bad disturbances in the deep mind. I know that the things I tell about may seem not so. I merely wish to present them in the way I am able to do, so that other persons may take what I offer for what it may

1754

be worth to them. I was not thinking to write out these things. I need to do that, for I have to have this little book as an appendix to another book.

Atoms too have a corona to them. Within that corona no self-activity is possible. Outside of that corona self-activity is possible. Press the coronas of the atoms close to the central nucleus and the atoms become changed atoms; maybe that is so. Nitrogen is not a very active chemical element at ordinary temperatures, and under ordinary atmospheric conditions. Maybe the coronas of those atoms that make up the molecules of atmospheric nitrogen are not just right. I think of some of the experiments in chemistry I myself did, when I was doing my college work. There is a nascent-stage atoms can get into. It is while they are in that state that they are most active.

Let us try to be ourselves (in our minds) atoms. We need to get the feeling of those very tiny ones. Maybe we can get good help if we try to imagine ourselves pressed upon from all sides, as you would be in a very bad panic - persons all piled up in a great struggling mass of terrified ones. What good do your frantic pushes do? You but make matters worse for the whole great struggling mass of persons. If everybody would be quiet, not move any at all - that is what I mean by the state within the atoms. In order for an atom to be an atom, myriads of very small particles of some kind of chemical-element have to be so pressed upon that no Brownian-movement is going on there within the atom, inside the shell that the Corona is. Brownian movement is caused by blows from thrilling particles that are in the space all about the tiny particle. Within the atoms, in that relatively big space that is all between the corona and the nucleus, no thrilling of any kind is going on. Thrilling is, I believe, some kind of self-movement. (Into this, I must not go in this little book. I have done much deep thinking into many things. I must be as brief in my book as I can be, so as to have it be clear, not confusing, and forceful.) Liquids and solids are states of matter due to something that has been done to the atoms that compose them; maybe that is so.

1755

We will now go to a consideration of crystal life on a grand scale. Continents grow. There is what might be called the cambium-region of continents, islands, and sea-bottoms. In the geology of the early rocks are evidences that what I have said about there being a crystal-kingdom of life-below the plant-kingdom is true. I will tell about some of those things. (I will have to go into a few of the details in this matter, for if any geologist should read this book, he would not believe me if he had no evidence in what I wrote that I knew about geology.) In the great sedimentary formations there are, in some of the beds, very many fossils. The ordinary fossils of the early forms are all examples of a partnership between small protoplasmic living cells, and living crystals. The whole Paleozoic formation is a demonstration of that fact. We ourselves can know that we human persons are having the benefit of the good partnership between protoplasm and crystal-life. All higher life has to base back on some form or forms of crystal life - for its necessary food and for help in some of its problems of body structure. How very many different kinds of small protoplasmic cells there are in the intestinal-tract of a human person. How very many tiny glands there are, each one lined with many special living cells. They are places where chemist-crystals live and do their wonderful work. Granules are in those cells. What are those granules? They are, actually, living crystals. The life of those tiny crystals can continue on indefinitely, because the size of the tiny crystal is kept down; it can keep on growing. As the crystal grows in some parts of it, it is used up by the protoplasm in other parts of it. During the period of digestion of food, the tiny crystals build themselves up to their largest size, then there is a resting state, while the protoplasm is using up some of that chemically-built protoplasm food. While the crystal is growing, it is living. The living it does goes on only while the crystal is growing. When it ceases that growing - that is like sleep.

Grains of sand are sleeping quartz-crystals. Put them into the right kind of solution of silicon, and the eroded places of the grain of sand fill out, so that the character-

1756

istic crystal the grain of sand originally was, has been reformed, from the part of a crystal that the grain of sand was. What is known as quartzite is rock that has been made up of sand that had, as it were, been waked up to grow again.

If you believe that quartzite grows (and what geologist can doubt that fact?), you have to believe that there is the crystal-kingdom of life. We who know geology know that all of the different kinds of silicates that go to make up granite, and other crystalline rocks, can form in aqueous solutions. Geology is full of the evidence of the growth of crystals of rocks from out of aqueous solutions. The assumed crystallization of the primitive rocks from out a molten magma is not at all necessary to the formation of the original rocks. (The geologists assumed that the earth was originally molten rock-material. So, believing that, they had to get their rock from that source.) Why not give up that idea of a molten rock-material? I myself did that years ago. How great a change that has made in my thinking about many things. All rocks crystallized out of very heavy aqueous-solutions many miles down in the one great ocean of aqueous solutions that is all beneath the sea-bottoms, continents, and islands, and float in that very heavy water, as iron floats in mercury. Continents are floating titanic masses of crystalline rocks. Originally all the many chemical-elements were in solution in the waters of the one great ocean. The separation of the various chemical-elements from the water of the great ocean was done by living crystals. No hot stage was there to the evolution of the earth. That is a mistake. Sun is not hot. Sun does not radiate heat out into space. How that idea seems to cling even in the minds of some of the scientists. They tell you "how hot it is at the surface of Sun". They calculate how much heat is given off from Sun every million years - so as to try to tell "how much longer sun will continue to be what we need for our living". "The dying sun", you see that idea in some books by prominent astronomers. How many billions of great stars there are. If all of them had been radiating heat out into space for millions of years, would

1757

not it be quite hot in space by now? Where does all that heat go? Of course the heat you feel when you are exposed to the rays of the sun is heat generated in place, by light-resistance, just as the heat in an electric-toaster is generated in place by electric resistance.

One more thing about the great sun. We see that there are great good effects of light. Light is what we all have to have. Plants are living beings that can do some wonderful things, by making good use of light. Living protoplasm has to have some light. All that activity that goes on in the green leaves of plants is not plant activity; it is crystal activity. The doing of the work that leaves were made for the purpose of doing has to be left to living crystals; all that the plant cells do is to make necessary arrangements so that the crystals will be supplied with the substances they need and the waste matter will be taken away, and the crystals themselves will not be let grow too large. The seeds of plants? What about them? Are they living tiny embryo plants? There is a sleeping state below the state we know as living. There, in that state, very tiny crystals "sleep".

How very much there is to all this. I have told about the deep sleep we know as death (the death sleep), in this book that I have written. I must not go into that in this appendix. I have to show the connectedness of the life of all beings.

In this little book I must go into some matters of geology. I have to go against what all the geologists of these times believe is assured geologic facts. So, I have to be somewhat thorough in what I write. To the ordinary person, geology may not be a thing that has much interest. But life is interesting to all thinking persons. It is some kind of records of ancient life that geology is about. My way of looking at all that makes you know that life is always what you have to think, if you go deep into anything you may be interested in.

In the year 1938, I think it was, a bad cyclone came to the New England States (to that part of the continent of North America). At that very time a seismograph in Sitka, Alaska, made a record of movements of the place, there in Sitka. I have seen no attempt by any scientist to explain that strange fact. I believe that fact was due to what I said about continents; they float in the great ocean that is beneath the sea bottoms and continents. That is my explanation of that fact. I give it for what it may be worth to you.

This morning I was reading in the big geology book about the so-called Arachean system of rocks. They were at one time thought to be the primary basal rocks of the earth's crust. It is said in the place I was reading, that the metamorphism caused by the pressure of the igneous rocks on the rocks that were above them was not merely due to pressure contact. Other facts than that fact of general pressure were factors in making the rocks be as they are known to be. All of those facts and very many more important ones, can be explained by great mountain-ranges growing up through some of the overlying beds of rocks. In a short book that is intended for ordinary persons who know little about geology, I must not load my writing with the many interesting things that geologist know about. The geologist may think I have not taken everything into consideration. Let me tell them that I have been working over twelve years, off and on, on what this short book for common ordinary readers is based back upon. I know geology. All those years I read and thought about problems of geology. With geologists I could go into many intersting details. I will make this statement for geologists to read and think into. If there were no fossils of original crystal life (fossils from the era of life before the plant fossils and the animal fossils appeared), how could the many great beds of limestone and dolomite be, that far down in the old sedimentary formations? Where did all that calcium carbonate come from? It is supposed to have come from shells. I believe that much of the limestone and dolomite are geologic records of the work of living crystals, living crystals that were not in any partnership with plant protoplasm, or animal protoplasm. I believe that there was a great era of life before there were any animals or plants, anterior to all that life that is well recorded by the cambrian beds of sedimentary rocks.

I believe that all crystalline rocks are geologic records of living crystals. Metamorphism was but a secondary change. We need to get the right idea about the original condition of matter after the earth had taken form. Was it a molten mass of rock materials? How could the earth have been that hot if it had been formed as the geologists seem to believe it was, hot enough so that even after millions of years the thick crust (that geologists assume is all about a very hot shrinking central region) could warp great hundreds-of-miles-long-regions up so as to peneplane it down, and then, after another million years, warp the same great long region far down again, so that the water of the sea could go there - so that the marine fossils of that one of the geologic periods could be deposited there to form, far inland in the continent, great continuous thick beds of fossils)? Great regions of the massive rocks did get raised high up and crumpled, of course. In the regions of great growing mountain ranges that was always so. That was not caused by a wrinkling of an assumed crust of the whole earth. That is merely local to that region caused by the growth upward of a mountain range. How much the geologists have labored - to try to make the observed facts of geology fit some theories they have come to believe in. This theory of a crust all about the whole earth is not true. How bad some of the theories of the scientists are for everybody. If the scientists had thought their way all the way through the science they were interested in, before they tried to tell people how things were, how much better that would have been for everybody. Some bad assumptions geologists have been burdened with for many years. This shrinking crust of a contracting earth is one of them. As I go my way along in this appendix, I will tell something about some of the other bad assumptions of the geologists.

I was writing a story from out a former cycle of my life, a cycle in which, I was a minstrel of my clan. (As minstrel, it was my work to know about all the good things that happened to persons of our clan and to some of the persons of other clans. Of course when minstrels from some other clan would come to your own settlement, some

1760

new stories would get passed along. I was not one who had much to do with many other minstrels, that cycle of my life. But there came to our clan a very old minstrel. He was much older than people get to be in these times. He was at least four hundred years old. He was not sure whether it was five centuries or only four. He told me about some very terrible great deep swift floods that had devastated the great Jungle-lands of Middle-America, long before his time; those stories of the very great floods had been handed down by many minstrels from very ancient times. I was astonished by all that. I had known about a lesser flood; but a flood that would come in from the level open ocean was a thing I could not understand. Neither could he understand it. We were not what most people of these times think the Indians of ancient times were, mere unintelligent brute-like cave-dwelling people; we thought about many things. Very great stone palaces were made in big settlements that were walled all about with good strong walls the joints of the great stones of which were very well done. All that required careful plans and accurate measurements. Very much of that accurate dressing of stone for great walls was done, very far back in ancient times. The people of these times do not seem to know how well all the things of those times were done. We owe very many of our best most useful ideas and ideals to the deep-thinkers of very ancient times. As minstrel of my clan, that cycle of my life, I got much from my being with that very old wise minstrel. He himself had to migrate, with a small part of the clan he was of, because of a small one of those floods that had come right in from the open ocean.) Years ago I began to try to get back enough from that cycle of my life so that I could make a good useful story of that. When I got to the flood - things began to happen to me. Already I was interested in geology; that had been one of the interests that I had kept up for years. Coming upon the story in which that smaller one of those sea-floods was, I thought into all that. That was what got me to doing, yet again, deep thinking down into geology. How much has come to me because of that much deep thinking. I would not have come to know about the great

1761

crystal-kingdom of life if I had not done that thinking into things of geology.

I have to give, in this appendix, some of the good reasons why I know that flood that I came upon, in one of my ancient Indian stories, actually happened. You see how it is with me, you thinking reader of this book. I am interested to try to do something worth while about the terrible age-old muss the whole human race is down in. To do that, I have to tell many things that I worked out in many former cycles of my long-life. But the people of these times do not believe in any long-life; they think that the present cycle of life is all there is, as far as they are concerned; (because they themselves do not recall things from out any former cycles of their life, they do not believe there ever were any of those; they have not heard anything about all that.) You see, I have many bad difficult problems always on my hands, as I write the kind of things I have to write. Usually I write stories, true stories from out some former cycle of the long-life of me. I am doing something different in this appendix. So much was there to explain about that flood that I took it out of that story so that I could do all the explaining, the much explaining that was necessary - so that people would know that the flood actually happened. Floods. How would I tell about only one flood and a relatively small one at that? I would have to explain the causes of those floods that came in from the open ocean, or people would think my story was only a made-up story.

How much I was helped in my trying to understand how ocean floods could be, when it came to me that originally rocks did not form from the cooling of molten rock material, but crystallized out of dense solutions very far down in the one great ocean that the earth essentially is. How very much deep thinking I had to do for years, all alone by myself (as I went about my work as a family doctor). How about water-of-crystallization? How could there be that in all crystalline rocks, if they had formed in the way the geologists say they were formed from molten rock material? Water in the form of hot water vapor might be in a molten mass of rock, if there was no way for

1762

the steam to get out; but would not there be many tiny holes in that rock, when the mass cooled - like pumice stone, something like that? Heat drives out water-of-crystallization. You can get entirely away from all the bother of that whole matter by believing the thing your eyes tell you if you are one who can think into what is written in big books of geology - all rocks were formed in the way you can see some rocks are formed (many kinds of them). Much of that goes on all the time, in cracks in the rocks; veins in rocks were all made that way. Crystallization out of aqueous solutions is the normal thing, the thing you would expect. Why then try to bring in all that about an assumed molten magma? Crystallization out of aqueous solutions was not secondary, as geologists assume; it was primary.

What would cause a great flood to come in from the sea? How would it be, if no rock was taken off from the top of a great growing up mountain range that had already grown high up out of the ocean? Crystallization on the very extensive bottom of the great range would not be equal in all places, miles down beneath the sea bottoms. A time might come when some part of the range would get to leaning over to one side or to the other. It is not hard to imagine that some part of the floating range might tip so far to one side that part of the great range would break off and tip over. What a great event that would be. What very great waves that would cause. But that would be only a minor thing, that thing in itself.

Of course you would need very much more than such a thing as that would be, to cause a great tidal wave, to come all up over the land for hundreds of miles. The tipping over of even one mountina could precipitate, cause to begin, very great floods all over the earth. See how things are all along all the sea coasts. Much material is washed down to the sea in a few hundred years. In very ancient times there were no sea bottoms anywhere; so the materials washed into the sea would sink very far down in the great ocean. They would go down till the heavy water down there would bear them up; they would float, suspended in the heavy water many miles down, next to the rock of the great

1763

keel of that great mountain range. Rocks in which silicon or lime get cemented together in great solid masses. In the course of several thousand years great wide extensive submarine shelves would be concreted to the sides of the titanic rock ship, as it floated there in the ocean. The soluble substances that are washed into the sea, they too would sink down into the water. Sand too would sink down. The greater the pressure, deep down in the ocean, the more easily rocks go into solution. Those rocks that went far down into the ocean would be partly dissolved. That would provided solutions that would act as fertilizers to make that mountain range grow up a little faster than otherwise it would grow up. All along the edges of great continents mountain ranges have grown up there where the fertilizer had been provided for them. In very ancient times that was caused by the going very far down into the water of the great ocean of much waste material that had been eroded off from the land. Nothing like the growth upward of mountain ranges that happened in very ancient times happen now. Why? Because now everywhere all over the whole deep ocean, covering it over, there are sea bottoms, in the regions between the continents and the islands; so that the waste materials that are eroded off from the land cannot any longer go down to where the active growing region of the continents are. In very ancient times the very great mountain ranges were like great wedges that were being forced up from below by the titanic power of very much growing crystalline rock. The power of growing crystals is a very great power. (How easily growing ice can break open a thick iron cannon, if the opening is stopped up.) Great continents were raised up by that tremendous power. We see, in a small way, something like that, when we see how the giant sequois are lifted up by the growth of the wood in them; all that great weight is held up by living wood, on the bottoms of the trees. If you are in the right mood for it, you can understand that all that is normal for the myriads of crystals that were born and grew up very many miles down in the one great ocean. They know nothing else but great pressure, know no lesser pressures.

1764

The submarine great wide extensive shelves, that reached many miles out from the sides of the great ship would break off if some unusual thing happened. That breaking off of the tremendously heavy region of the submarine shelf would start the great ship to rocking. That would break off many great shelves and so would make the great ship rock all the more. More and more great regions of the great wide projecting submarine ledges would break off. That will get you to see how very great long-continued tidal waves would come in from the ocean. That thing, once started, affected the great ocean everywhere all over the earth. Great submarine shelves would break off of the other continents. Titanic floods of deep sea water would wash all across all the land. That would continue for many weeks. Very much cutting down of the surface of the land would be done, in a few weeks' time. Great deep canyons and gorges and sea channels would be cut out quickly. Great long-continued earthquakes would shake up the beds of rocks in very many places. Volcanoes would spout forth. A very great earth-wide cycle of geologic change would take place in a few weeks' time. Great extensive thick strata of unsorted and later sorted, materials would be laid down by titanic floods.

That great thing was necessary to that kind of growth, crystal-kingdom growth. Get that into your mind. Only by taking off much weight from the continent could the living of the myriads of crystals continue on, many miles down in the great ocean, there on the great bottom of the titanic ship made of crystalline rock. The kind of life crystals live requires that the dead crystals be taken away from the living part of the mass. What to us seems like a titanic catastrophe was to the great continent "a great good relief", and a new awakening to renewed growth.

In one of the big books of geology that I have, I came across years ago, a thing I wish you to read and think about. (At that time, thinking to use that quotation in a book that I hoped to get published then, I got the permission of the publishers of that Geology to use that in my book. So, I feel free to give that in this appendix.

"Nearly one-half of North America was buried in ice.

1765

Strangely enough, it was not strictly the northern half, but the northeastern half that was specially ice-invaded, and, more strangely still, not so much the mountainous portions, though these were affected, as the plains. Alaska was largely free from ice, except in or about the mountains; and continuous glaciation did not extend as far south on the mountain girt plateaus of the Pacific border as on the smooth low plains of the Mississippi valley. Much the greater part of the 4,000,000 square miles of the ice fields lay on the plains of Canada and in the upper Mississippi valley. The Missouri and Ohio rivers, like two great arms, embraced the borders of the greatest of the ice sheets to which they owe their origin....

"One of the most marvelous features of the ice dispersion was the pushing out of the great Keewatin sheet from a low flat center, without a suggestion of a mountain nucleus, 800 to 1000 miles westward and southwestward over what is now a rising semi-arid plain, while mountain glaciation on the west, where now known, pushed but little beyond the foothills." (Geology by Chamberlin and Salisbury - Henry Hold & co.)

Athwart the long northeastern coast of Canada for two thousand miles, high Greenland with its northern extension, high Ellesmere Land, stretches its long high length. The southern end of Greenland, on the one hand, and long high Labrador with its extension (the island, Newfoundland), on the other hand, make a great funnel, you might say, leading into great Baffin Bay. (Get a good atlas, so you can follow me, as I tell about this.) Off the mouth of that great funnel lie Newfoundland Banks, a very extensive one of those submarine shelves I told about. A great extensive region of that broke off, and sank. That started one of those titanic geologic cycles of great erosion. When that great thing got well started, great bore after great bore after great bore rushed roaring up that hundreds-of-miles ong great funnel - the great bores cumulating in height, and consequently in force, till they got up into great Baffin Bay. What a titanic force-pump that was, that hundreds-of-miles long great funnel, when worked by those continuing great piston-like

1766

bores. Very much, very deep, very swift water has a different higher order of power than that of an ordinary flood. All that water had to go somewhere. For weeks that would continue on. Up over high Greenland some of that flood water rushed. How wide was the titanic waterfall that was there for a thousand miles or more. That flood water too had to go somewhere, go somewhere in the ocean east of great Greenland. It made a great wide kind of a river in the ocean. Two such very wide great rivers in the Arctic ocean were formed. One went east of the north pole, the other went west of it. Where the two great streams met, there north of Russia - that flood water also had to go somewhere. It flooded down across Siberia, and on southward.

That was but some of the spillings-over of the titanic flood that was rushing very swiftly up into great Baffin Bay. Greenland, and high Ellesmere Land were a kind of a titanic deflector of the main stream of that titanic continuing flood of very deep, very swift heavy sea water. (I believe that the water from very far down in the ocean, a hundred miles or more down, is very different from the water we know about. I said something about the coronas that I believe are about each atom. If the atoms of the molecules of water are compressed very much, I believe that the coronas would be tight up against the nuclei of the atoms. I believe that kind of water would be very much heavier than ordinary water is, and would have very much greater solvent power. Do not get the idea that heavy water would change back suddenly to ordinary water when it came up to the surface of the ocean. It is a permanent change that has taken place in those atoms.)

The main stream of the titanic floods fanned out from that thousand-miles-long great high deflector. Look at the atlas; see how that was. Southward, southwestward, westward and northwestward the great floods rushed. Very deep was that sea water. Deep water, when it is going very swiftly, can carry very great rocks along in it. And it can push much heavier great rocks along on the beds of rock. That pushing of very many great many-hundreds-of-tons heavy rocks along on the smoothed beds of rock is what ground fine the very much rock of which practically all of the sedimentary rocks of interior North America were made from. It was those very great rocks pushed along on the smooth bedrock that did all of the planing down of all northwestern Canada - in the very ancient time when no other land was anywhere up out of the ocean. There were many of those titanic floods; they recurred in eras of the past. I believe that great Greenland, and the region of Canada that lies west of that, was the first part of the continent of North America to show up above the water of the ocean; all that kept growing up out of the ocean in eras of the past. I believe that nearly all of the sedimentary rocks that were laid down anywhere in North America came from there; that was the continuing source of supply of ground-up rock. And how very much dissolved material must have resulted from all that grinding fine of very much rock. The Rocky Mountains grew up under great thick beds of sedimentary rocks. Where did all that enormous amount of ground-up rock come from? The geologists do not seem to have seen the greatness of all that; they do not see the thing whole. All across the thousand miles to the eastern flanks of the Rockies the ancient floods rushed. Before there were any mountains there in the west, similar great deep floods had swept all across the whole great continent. It was the going far down into the great deep ocean of very much of that broken up rock, sand, and dissolved rock material that made the Rocky Mountains grow up there. The geologists do not see the thing whole.

Where much sediments go miles down (into the one great ocean that earth is, essentially,) continents, or islands, or sea-bottoms grow up. The edges of continents are often lined with chains of mountain ranges. Those ranges of mountains were faster growing parts of the slowly growing continent. Those places, many miles down in the liquid soil out of which continents grow, were fertilized, you might say, by all those waste-products that had sunk down there, so that edge of the continent grew up to form mountain ranges. (The greater the pressure in the deep ocean, the more the rock is dissolved.)

Floods of sea water, many titanic floods of deep very

1768

swift sea water (not ice moving a mere foot a day), are what did all that very much eroding down of the slowly growing up continent. The longer the geologists hold to that glaciation theory, the more trouble they will have with it. When your basal theory is wrong, you have continual trouble trying to make the observed facts fit the wrong theory. When your basal theory is right, you are more and more satisfied with it. We are told that there were great extensive ice sheets even back before there was any evidence of life in the earth. We are told that extensive ice sheets lay on low plains in India, part of them within the tropics. How such thick extensive ice sheets could make all the thick sedimentary beds of the earth is a thing the geologists can never explain. How figs and magnolias could be far up in the northern part of North America, though many great thick ice sheets had been there (very much more ice there for millions of years than anywhere else in the earth, outside of polar regions), the geologists do not tell us. They know surely that those magnolias and figs did grow that far north. They can only assume all that about continuous glaciation. Why do they not start from sure facts and go from there? Are there any surer facts of geology than beds of fossils are?

Ice does not melt from the mountains in the tropics at all; it stays there all the year around. How very hot, then, must have been the climate to melt the assumed miles-thick ice-sheet that covered four million square miles of northeastern North America in Pleistocene times? How peculiar it was that so very much more snow fell there in eras of the past, than fell anywhere else in the earth, not in the polar regions. The geologists have to try to explain that. No mountains were anywhere there. The geologists are not daunted; they are ready with another theory to show that the thing could be done. What caused the extreme change in climate from ice-epoch to very hot inter-glacial period? Are there any evidences in the fossil-beds of the earth to show that there were ever any such very great changes in climate?

In the beds of Silurian fossils are corals. Corals like

1769

warm seas. In the northern part of Canada can be found those kinds of fossils. I am one who cannot be credulous enough to believe in all that glaciation-business of the geologists. I need to feel sure about the basal theories of any science I study deeply down into. I am not, of course, an authority in geology, or in anything else. I am ready to be shown, if I am wrong, in this matter.

In order to get the full force of the truth that it was titanic floods of very deep very swift sea water that did most of the cutting down of the continent, as it grew slowly up, I must try to get you to see, in your mind, what was happening in the region of northeastern North America at the time of one of those great floods. I have told of the titanic continuing deep floods that kept coming up the hundreds-of-miles-long great funnel into great Baffin Bay. That great bay did not just happen to happen there. It had to be dug out. How did the thick ice do that? How did the ice cut Ellesmere Land off from Greenland? How did the thick ice, within the Arctic region, cut out all those many great long wide sea-channels that are there at the north-top of the great wide continent? Those many channels in Arachean rock were cut out. What was the titanic force, the continuing very great force in great thick ice sheets lying at sea level to do all that? It seems silly to ask such questions. But, practically everybody believes in the Glacial Periods. If there is any person who does not believe in that, I have not yet heard of him. (I have talked to no persons outside my own family about this matter. I have talked to no geologist about all this; all I know of what geologists believe is what I have read in the best books of geology we now have.)

One good thing the geologists did, in all that northeastern part of North America. They hunted out very many direction-giving glacial-markings all over that whole very great region, so as to get some idea in which directions the assumed ice flowed out from the centers of ice-dispersion. Those maps they made based on that work, give you a good idea of the directions in which the last great floods fanned all out, from the very long high great deflector I spoke of. It is not a good thing to be too sure of those directions, however,

1770

for they were based on very many short direction-giving markings on the bed-rock. You have the feeling that was an attempt to make the facts fit the moving-ice assumption.

I do not have to depend on such unsure geologic evidence as that is. Look at the Atlas. See how relatively straight the eastern shoreline of great Hudson Bay is. From the top of Foxe Basin to the bottom of James Bay the line is relatively straight. That direction-giving line is about thirteen hundred miles long. I believe that very long relatively straight shoreline is a sure great geologic record of the direction of the main stream of the titanic floods that rushed very swiftly southward there, in Pleistocene times.

I look somewhat west of south on the map. There the big bulge of very great Hudson Bay is. What made all that? It did not just happen to happen to get there; it had to be gouged out of hard Archean rock. Off beyond that great bulge southwestward lies Lake Winnipeg, no small geologic record in itself. Beyond it lies yet another long Lake. Floods rushing westward did all that.

How very many lakes there are in all that part of Canada. I am not a field geologist, so I have not visited about in that part of Canada. I see what looks to me like good geologic evidence on the map I have of that vast region. The streams show you surely the lay of the land there. The many lakes had to be cut out of Archean rocks, or cut out of rocks that former great floods had laid down there. (The later floods worked over what former floods had left there. Floods were the geologic agents of all that. Great very extensive thick strata of rocks were laid down by great floods even in Proterozoic times.) Where I see a great lake, or a great bay, I think a titanic Maelstrom must have been while the titanic deep swift floods were doing their very great geologic work. Baffin Bay, Hudson Bay, the five Great Lakes, Lake Winnipeg, Reindeer Lake, Lake Athabaska, Great Slave Lake, and Great Bear Lake, are, I believe, sure geologic records of Maelstroms of the very great deep swift floods of ancient times. You can see from the map how, while very much deep swift floodwater was being deflected southward, by that great long high deflector, other titanic deep swift floods were rushing westward from the great funnel directly into Hudson Bay. Would not that make a very great continuing Maelstrom there? Would not that cut out very great regions of rock in a short time? It takes a titanic geologic agent to make a titanic geologic record.

The geologists do what seems to me to be a very unscientific thing; they make use of a geologic agent that is very much too weak to do the given very great geologic work, and give that too weak geologic agent millions of years to do that work in. If the geologic agent is too weak for that geologic work, then no matter how many millions of years you give it, it cannot do that work. Could a small ant move a ten-pound rock if you gave him ten millions of years to do that in? Geologists see a stream rushing in the bottom of a deep canyon. It is as if they said to you: "See, the stream did all that." They would go on to say, "Of course it took very many centuries for it to cut its way that far down into the rock. But we know that each year it does a little cutting out of rock. Add up the many littles, and there you are. You have to get used to thinking 'millions of years', if you are to understand geology. This that you see here, this deep canyon in the mountains, is a 'young valley'. Come here after several millions of years, and all this great region will be what geologists call a 'peneplane'." Geologists believe that. They believe that ordinary rain-erosion, freezing-water erosion, running stream-erosion, shore-line erosion, and wind-erosion, cut great ranges of high mountains down to what they call a base level. They believe that there are cycles of that kind of general erosion, cycles that would require, they say, millions of years of time. The mountains rise up again in some weak place of the earth's crust, rise up high. That starts another cycle of that general very slow erosion. They do not seem to think that the deep canyon, or gorge, might have been cut out before the small stream came there. They see a mighty river of ice in a great gorge in mountains. They see it pushing, very slowly (on an average maybe not more than a foot a day), some rocks and gravel down, or carrying some of that on its back. They show you parallel striae, or grooves in the rock of the great bed of the glacier. They take it for granted that the moving ice cut out all that great deep groge. They do not seem ever to think that the gorge could have been there before any ice formed there. Great deep swift floods can do, very much better, and ever so much quicker, any of the geologic work great glaciers can do and much more. All that very great deposit of what geologists believe is glacial till or glacial drift, could have been laid down by great deep swift floods. The very great erratic bowlders, as the geologists call them, hundreds-of-tons heavy great rocks that have been carried maybe several hundreds of miles from the ledges from which they must have come, in some cases carried up hundreds of feet above the level of the place from which they were taken, could easily have been transported there by one of those great swift deep floods. The very much unsorted waterworn material of the so-called glacial-drift is, I believe, sure geologic evidence of swift floods. Swift deep water does not sort the material it lays down. The much grooving of the bedrock and of the transported rocks, and the making of the many parallel striae, could have been done by swift floods.

You do not have to lower great extensive regions of continents very gradually down low enough so that the sea can come there, in order to get beds of marine fossils far from the normal coasts of the continent. Great deep swift floods of sea water could do all that in a few weeks' time. The distribution of the characteristic fossils of the geologic periods after the Paleozoic period show, I believe, that swift floods of sea water swept across from that great deflector to the eastern flanks of the Rockies. Get a big geology that shows the distribution of the fossils of the various geologic periods. Look at the places where the fossils of the given periods are to be found, in interior North America. Look at all that thoughtfully; in the great Cretaceous floods, the fossils were laid down along that far region at the eastern flanks of the Rockies in a band from the Gulf of Mexico to the Arctic Ocean. Some of the flood water rushed through some of the passes in the Rockies of Canada. The hundreds-of-miles long narrow lakes in the stream-bed of the Columbia River are, I believe, good geologic evidence of that fact. The distribution of the beds of the Queen Charlotte series of fossils is, I believe, geologic evidence that those fossils were swept there from the Atlantic Ocean, and deposited in the several separated places where they now can be found. They are clastic fossils. The very great extent of gravel terraces in the great gorge of the Columbia and in the gorge of the Fraser, are, I believe, good geologic evidence that there gravel-carrying floods, rushing down from the mountains, met great floods that had come in from the Pacific. Where the speed of the floods was suddenly checked, there the gravel would be laid down. I can think of no other cause for that much gravel being there. How very deep some of those gravel deposits are, in some cases two or more hundred feet thick.

What made the many great planes of unconformity was great deep swift floods, not the peneplaning of the geologists, or their continuous glaciation. What would take that slow general erosion process millions of years to do (if it could do all that), a great deep swift flood could do in maybe a month. The time that the various planes of unconformity were some kind of a measure of, was time from one great flood to the next one. Maybe the plane of unconformity, the bed of unsorted waterworn material, the sorted finer material, from gravel to fine sand, might have been made by the same flood; for at first so swift would be the flood water that no material would be laid down; much cutting down of the bedrock would be done; then, the speed of the water slackening, unsorted materials would come down, then, the water going more slowly, the material would be sorted. The floods might come in great cumulations, to be followed by a period of less depth of flood, a repetition of such action. If that was the case, several great planes of unconformity would be made at about the same time. Another thing that you should have in your mind. The geologists seem to believe that all sedimentary formations were laid down level, or on a not-steep slope, as if they

1774

were all sedimented out of ordinary not swift water. Great deep swift floods would lay down thick layers of material up against the steep slope of a mountain range. The much cross-bedding was done by such floods. If a geologist finds the same kind of sedimentary beds on each side of a mountain range, he takes it for granted that the sedimentary bed was, when it was laid down, a continuous one, all up over that range. So he shows, on his geologic map of that region, how the sedimentary bed must have been all up over that range, pushed up, and then eroded off where the range of the mountain was. That the same kind of sedimentary material might have been deposited each side of that range of mountains at about the same time seems not to be thought of by geologists. They seem to have to believe in the wrinkling of an assumed crust of the earth to conform with a contracting cooling hot interior region of the earth; as if the rocks were in layers all over the earth.

The fossils of the many geologic periods and main divisions of periods, after the very early ones were, I believe, laid down by great deep swift floods, or were sedimented from great inland salt lakes that had been left by some of those great floods. Deposits of salt over four thousand feet thick in Germany speak for an ancient great deep inland salt lake there. Great deposits of salt are found in many regions of the continents of the earth. I cannot see how those can be accounted for by any slow emergence of the great region up from out the sea (after it had been slowly lowered down, as the geologists suppose). The very slowness of that would tend to make a great swamp there. How then would there be almost pure salt there, in very great deep thick deposits? Dry desert conditions could not be, for the sea would be right there all the time that the land was rising slowly up. A great deep swift flood could sweep a very great amount of sea water far into the middle of a great dry desert, and leave it there, to dry up quickly. (The dry-lakes of the desert regions of western United States were, I believe, made in that way. To speak of what might seem to be a little thing, I believe that the many desert turtles, turtles that have evolved since ancient times so that they are able to go without water for many months at a stretch, by feeding on green desert browse, are an evidence of those same great floods; I believe they were salt-water turtles from some great ancient inland salt sea, left by a great flood of sea water. How much smaller they are now than the marine turtles we know about. This is only my own thought about that; I am not competent to say whether my idea is a true one.)

This is a kind of a condensed summary of things I wrote out, several times. It is not in a very good order; I have given it as it came to me, while I wrote. I have gone over the whole matter yet again, recently, to see if, maybe, I was mistaken about the matter of those great deep swift floods of sea water. How many times I have gone into this matter, a matter that is interesting to me. Each time I find yet more important things to confirm me in my belief that I am right in all this. Until recently I had not thought much of the earlier floods. I was interested recently to find that the geologists believe that very extensive continuous glaciation took place in the southern hemisphere in very early times in permian times. Australia was very much glaciated according to the geologists. Much so-called glacial drift has been found in Australia, in Tasmania, in India, in South Africa, and in South America. The geologists are much puzzled by all this. Yet, they still cling to that belief in what they call continuous glaciations.

One time, many years ago, I lived for a while in what is known as the Musselshell-region of Montana. We were on the edge of what we called the bad-lands. Many big fossils were there, weathering on the surface of the ground. You knew that they had not ever been covered up. They were, I believe, Triassic, or Jurassic, Ammonites. They were like great snail-shells, some of them as much as a foot and a half across. The shell material was still there, had not been changed by being covered up with rock; they were not bedded in the rock at all. You would see a clump of what looked like broken rock. You would go there and would see that it was one of those weathered big Ammonite shells. How pretty some of them were. Where the partitions of the

1776

many small rooms of the interior of the big shell met the surface of the shell, the line of union could be seen, a sinuous line. There were too in that region very many other big fossils that had been covered with only a few feet of loose sandy material. In the cuts a new railroad had made I saw very many of those. Some of the fossils may have been the lower solid portions of Jurassic belemnites. Only about thirty miles west of that region, on the plains, were some beds of fossil-leaves. A thick mass of fossil-leaves like maple leaves was there. The rock seemed to be nothing but those fossil leaves. Near that place were coal mines that were not deep mines; the coal was near the surface of the plains. It seems to me that the place there might have been at the extreme western reach of a Jurassic flood. Much forest material would have been carried that thirty miles farther on than the heavy Ammonite shells would be carried. Of course geologists probably know all about all that; and may laugh at me. I am, as I said, no authority. But as the saying is, "A cat can look at a king".

I must tell something about the formations that can be found east of the mountain range that is the eastern rim of North America. It is to me an interesting confirmation of what I have said about great deep swift floods of sea water, in eras of the past. It is only a little that I will say about that. Geologists do not know how to account for what they call the Newark Series of formations of the Triassic System of rocks. It was not hard for me to see how those formations could have been laid down. Great deep floods sweep along with them much solid material. The swifter the flood, the bigger the pieces of rock. It is deposited, if the speed of the flood is sufficiently checked. Floods came down the eastern coast of North America from the flooded St. Lawrence Valley, at the time of one of those titanic floods; that valley could by no means hold all that. The Catskill formations and the Newark formations were laid down by those spillings-over from out the overflowing St. Lawrence Valley, in eras of the past. See how that was. How few fossils there are in the Catskill formations. How few fossils there are in the Newark formations. How singular that is, for those formations are not far from the ocean. (How full of fossils the formations are that were formed by sedimentation from the water of the ocean, under normal conditions.) Only after the many fossils had been swept far onward, during the great flood, were any materials of the Catskill formations, or the Newark formations, laid down. That fact, the fact that there are few fossils in those sedimentary rocks, seems to me to be good geologic evidence of titanic flood action.

Another thing. Much limestone conglomerate is in the Newark formations. It, the much limestone, could have been transported there from far up in Canada. (No near source of all that broken up limestone has been discovered.)

I leave this whole matter in this unfinished state, here in this appendix. I could write a book about the interesting things I have thought into, along this line. How good it is to have good wholesome interests all the time, interests that grow, the more you live with them. Eskers - how much fun I have had in my thinking about those geologic records. The material of them is unsorted waterworn material. Parts of the great queer snakes may lie on what had been swamps. Maybe the snake lies with part of his long body up on low hills. To me, that means the place where the great waves of a big flood went up the temporary beach and then ran back down, did that for a long enough time to make that characteristic kind of an embankment. Eskers in the region just south of the eastern ones of the Great Lakes, in Maine, in the British Isles, in Scandinavia? Think about that, with floods in your mind.

In one of the largest fresh water lakes of the earth there are fresh water seals. Fresh water sponges are there. Deep sea fishes are there. What do the geologists say about that? They think that sometime that lake must have been connected with the ocean. What a lot of trouble they go to about that. They have some theories that they believe in. It seems to be that those theories close their minds to any new ideas. Great lake Baikal, not far north of the Gobi Desert, confirms what I said about great floods of sea water rushing across Russia from the north. How easily the flood-theory, as I have

1778

outlined it, takes care of everything.

The chalk cliffs of Dover - how did they get there? One can be clear in one's mind about the wide distribution of fossil beds of the Cretaceous period, if one knows about the titanic deep floods that occurred in that era. So deep down was the water of the seas disturbed that time, that enormous quantities of globigerian ooze were carried in the flood water. Great floods coming in from the Atlantic met great floods coming down from the north through the North Sea. Where they met the force of the water was checked; there the water laid down its burden (where the Dover chalk cliffs of England are). To me it is a significant thing that the tiny fossils of the chalk deposits are clastic fossils.

On thing I must do, before I leave the matter of those floods. "Why do great floods not occur now? If floods occurred in eras of the past, will any flood come in these times? I must go into that matter. I have said that to the ancient living crystals (those ones that lived hundreds of miles down in the great ocean) those great cycles of geology that unloaded them from much of the mountain-load that they had to live under was necessary, normal. How great a change took place when the land grew up to the surface of the ocean. Light and air and lessened pressure did great things for some new kinds of living crystals, that period of the evolution of life in the earth. See that great thing whole, in your mind. We need to be thinking great thoughts, if we are thinking about great old good mother-earth. Who is it that said the stars sing? "Music of the Spheres", that kind of a thing. I believe that is so. I know that things do sing. Each thing has a characteristic tone to it. Would it be a tone if it was not continually singing? Gravity, that force, is due to the characteristic tone of great Mother-earth. She is, of course, a living person. I do not refer to the mere body she lives in (though parts of that are living, good useful crystal-life). All really great things are living beings, persons. In the mind of the invisible person is some work the person is interested in doing. The continuing interest in that gets done the things that need to be done, so that the invisible person will have the necessary tools to work with. (The mind grows

1779

a suitable body, as its instrument to work with.)

Mother earth had come to a great new era of her life. Before that time she had been interested in the kind of children (crystal-children) who knew how to grow far down in the ocean, be pressed upon by the great weight, and respond to that. Look at a piece of freshly-fractured granite. That is actually a part of a fossil bed; what you see are fossils of tiny beings that were once living beings; (while they were growing, those crystals were living). There are a a number of different kinds of crystals in any kind of granite. That is Paleozoic formation for you. You can be sure those fossils developed in place.

I must halt the doing of what I was working at to say a little about the deductions of geologists from what they have found in beds of fossils. Think of this paragraph as being within parenthesis marks. How much geologists make of the geologic evidence they get from the fossils of the fossil-beds. They have it all worked out - "ancient history of the evolution of life in this planet". What would you say to that if you knew that the shell you had found in place, in Triassic formation in Montana, had been carried there from off in the Atlantic ocean? The geologists take it for granted that the thing had that for its place to live in, before it became a fossil. They believe that the fossils of a given fossil-bed evolved together. Big mistakes have been made by the geologists. They believe in the evidence they get from beds of fossils - sometimes. How could there have been any plants in northern North America at all, if the ground were all covered miles deep with ice over a region that is mapped out by geologists as being the region of great concentrations of ice, during millions of years in many eras of the past? Many long ice-epochs they say have been. How then could figs and bananas and magnolias be in the ancient history of all that? The fossil beds up near the Arctic Circle give the lie to all that glaciation theory the geologists have got everybody to believe in. Ancient history is important. Geologists have demonstrated well their unfitness to decipher it.

To go back to old invisible mother-earth. She had thought

1780

that all her children would have to be like the primitive ones were - granite-crystal-children. Up near the surface of the ocean the pressure was not nearly as great as it is down where the first life was born, by mother-earth. Graphite too is crystalline. Lime-rock is crystalline. Dolomite, that magnesium and calcium carbonate, is crystalline. Quartz is crystalline.

How busy Mother-earth (the invisible person) must have been when the land had grown up to and a little above the water of the ocean. Now, you reader of this appendix, be wanting to know how things were far down in the dark depths of the great ocean. How about those babies of the old good mother? She had, of course, good thought for them. I will come to that. Of course when a mother finds out that there is a very much better place than the old one to be born in and grow up in, she would want all her children to migrate there. Granite-crystals could die and maybe come up into next cycles of life as carbon-compounds.

For a long period of time the land was low-lying land. Practically all the water there was salt water. (It is unfortunate that we think of ocean-water as being only that "sodium-chloride" water. It has other things in it. Out up from the ocean all the substances we have in the earth have come - (except a little that has come to us from abroad from time to time). Gases dissolve in sea water. (At first, very long ago, Earth was only a titanic mass of many different kinds of gases - decomposition products of the source-gas, ether. Water was the first gas to liquefy. Into that liquid water went gas after gas.) Solids came only when the first crystal was born, far down in the one great ocean of aqueous-solutions of many different kinds of substances - that rich liquid soil. Continents islands and sea bottoms grew in that soil. Growing crystals pushed up the titanic weight of the great continents, in eras of the past. That is, now in these times, pretty much ancient history. I believe that after the sea bottoms closed in all the deep ocean, so that no longer fertilizing material could go down there, that type of crystal life began to be obsolete, in this planet. New times, new kinds of ways of living. Crystals too are living the long-life.

Mother-earth was very busy, at the surface of her great body, trying out many growing experiments. It was the thing to make good provision for the coming up into next cycles of life of the many granite-crystals that had gone into the death sleep. (Forget not to think "invisible person" each and every time I write the words "living being". The substances of the body are of little importance, when you think of the principles of living those tiny material particles have to dance to the tune of.)

How interesting to the great mother all that was. Millions of small crystal-gardens in the air and sunlight made her much good interesting work to do. The thing was to find some way by which the cycles-of-life could be made longer. (How short are the cycles of life of the ferns that grow on the window, in the cold winter.) All that had to be thought out, actually worked out in the mind of some actual person. Earth is, actually, an invisible thinking person. Would you expect me to do any arguing about that?

How great a discovery it was, when mother-earth found that crystals of some kinds of carbon-compounds could keep on growing in parts of them, while the material of the mass that had already been made there, by that crystallization, was being dissolved away. It was one of the greatest discoveries she ever made. Plants and animals are the result of that good discovery. (Of course in a short account such as this is I cannot go into all this. I have said enough to get you to know how very great are the yet unexplored regions of the great good important science of geology.)

One more thing I must do. I was to show you whether any more titanic floods would come. No. A strange remarkable great vicious circle was broken, at the time of the Cretaceous floods. Before that time in northern North America, the main stream of the titanic floods returned much of the flood water right back to the place in the ocean it had gone ashore from (by way of the great St. Lawrence Valley), so that titanic quantities of washed-away rocks and sand were loaded on the great submarine shelf that Newfoundland Banks were. So, you see, each great flood made it a sure

1782

thing that another one of those great catastrophes would happen later on; the accumulation of weight of all that would, in time, break off another great region of that great continental submarine shelf, precipitating yet another one of those earth-wide geologic catastrophes. A great barrier, near to the south of the Great Lakes, was, at long last, done away with, by the great Cretaceous floods. After that, the much flood-water of the main-stream of those floods was spread out down into the great Mississippian region. (Before that time only great spillings-over from the floods got into what was, in Paleozoic times, a great long wide sheltered extension northward of the Gulf of Mexico. What is known as the Paleozoic sedimentary formations there, even those were not made up of the remains of sea-beings that had the Mississippian sea as their former home to evolve in; some of those were carried there by floods. The much good patient work of the paleontologists will have to be done over again, some of that work. Those planes of unconformity that geologists know about in those Mississippian Paleozoic sedimentary formations, are good geologic evidence of the spillings-over from titanic floods that, in those times, were not let rush in main force there. If that had been, no sedimentary formations would be there now, of Paleozoic times.) After that barrier had been cut away by the Cretaceous floods, the water spread out widely, and flowed down into the Gulf of Mexico. The vicious-circle was broken. No more of those great floods will come.

There is a Crystal Kingdom of life. You do not need to take my word for that. Do this. Go visit some home where there is a pretty little young attractive girl. Maybe you have one of your own. Watch what happens when she gets the very thing she has long wished for, dreamed about. Delight is sure evidence of the fact that myriads of tiny thrilling living crystals are all aquiver with increased stepped-up thrilling. No nerve-action there. The face of the child shines. She feels that even in her bones. It is all through her all at once. That is one thing.

What is awe? Have you ever thought of that? Things like that have to have a cause. Awe does not get done in you

1783

because of any nerves. All of the millions of tiny living crystals are with some sudden change in the kind of thrilling of them - all of them at the same instant. In the times of great sudden emergency, instantly each and every cell of your body knows just what to do. It is not nearly as complicated as that might seem to you to be. Things thrill. Tiny particles of the ever-present ether respond to that thrilling. There is no limit to the number of different kinds of messages the ether can carry, all at the same time. There is no interference at all, in that. It is a very remarkable thing. It is a known scientific fact. You have a radio crystal set of your own, a very remarkable one.

Tone - good body tone. Heath - what is that? "Tonics", taken to get you into better health. Think into those old words. I was wondering how it would be if I would make the end of this appendix be with a short ancient Indian story. It is not too much to tell you that no small thing ever happened to you (whoever you are who now are reading this last part of this appendix), that did not make some change in you, the PSYCHE you are, in the long-life of you. Those changes are in you, as a part of you; you have them in your mind. You have grown your mind all down the ages of the long-life of you. Get that in your mind. Each small happening that you lived through in some former cycle of your life is there, as a small part of that growth. The deep mind of you is an invisible growth. You do not see that. Do you see the not-good-thing, the cigarette habit of many millions of human people? You see what I mean; there are very many complicated things that no seen things can be the message-bearer of.

My story is this: "Do you want to be in my way?" He looked at me. The great old bear seemed to know what I meant. He was not just sure what to answer to that, so he sat down there. The trail was narrow. Brush was there. I was in no haste, that morning, but he was much better able to make a way for himself at the side of the brushy trail than I was. I was a small young Indian boy. He was not wanting to get out of my way. I was not wanting to get out of his way. (Of course, in those times, there was manners in

1784

that; those meetings on narrow places of trails were very common.) We considered the thing together, that morning. "I have heard," I said, "that the big one always makes way for the little one. How about that? Are you the big one, or am I?" He looked at me. He was with a good kind face. (He was one I had not seen there before. Six bears had our settlement for their home at that time. This one was not one of the six.)

"Who are you, anyway? Have you any right to come here? Who told you you could come take some of the things our six bears have as theirs? We have trouble enough already getting good things for the six. You make me kind of mad." I looked at him.

"We don't want any more great growly big-eaters in our settlement. You get away! Turn around and go!" I stood there. I looked him right in the puzzled eyes. He was no more afraid of me of course than he would have been of a lizard. He still sat there. I picked up a small stick and hit him on the sensitive nose with it. He growled. I held my ground. He was one who knew something about Indians. He knew that he must not do bad to any one of them. He was an old one. You knew by the looks of him that he was with good wiseness. He got up. He was not wanting to do that. He sniffed. He was, I thought, not going to mind me. I hit him again with all my small might. My stick made the blood come on his nose.

He would not be in any small doing. He thought that to fight so small a one as I was was against this dignity. He turned, and went fast back on that trail.

That is my story. That thing actually happened. It was the changing of the kind of thrilling first of the millions of tiny living crystals of my own body, and then the doing that to his many millions of crystals, that I had to do. I did that. You see what I mean. It is a very great important discovery in deep practical-psychology.

1785

LETTERS

FROM THE READERS

Where pertinent information concerning The Shaver Mystery is solicited from those who may have facts of value to offer.

Dear Sir:

Repeating what I want you mainly to grasp about the new work: With growth - a steady uninterrupted growth - life progresses swiftly to ever higher summits of achievement - and of value to the unit of life organization, the state and its citizen.

But, on earth the sun age poison causes a useless repetition of this growth - over and over - perhaps what the ancients meant sometimes by "ro", in truth not progress, but repetition.

Any step taken against this nullifying radioactive material will result in some true forward achievement by men.

Without it all our progress is pure illusion. Please see this.

On the story clip I sent you called Twilight - you must remember that they have had and lived with the antique mech for thousands of years like the people in Twilight - it works - never stops. BUT in time the mental generation of mental growth force fills with radioactive particles and causes a detrimental force to take control. The dero are the product of this effect - an hereditary monster that seems to be a man but definitely is not - is a Horla - and he exists in some numbers. And like the people of Twilight, the others have forgotten the necessity of effort toward safety or any struggle for life. This is hard to grasp as a present condition that ruins all earth life until you actually run up against it. I know you do not yet understand or believe much in the general existence of mad ray dero, but I

1786

assure you - when you learn from actual contact - you will wish you hadn't. There is no way I can tell you so you will grasp the truth of this matter, but I think if you diligently question men who seem to have trouble, or men like psychiatrists who go over mental troubles with patients, you will find a wealth of corroboration in what they have told the psychiatrist. Ask spiritualists of the apparitions, etc., if you want to establish this truth in your own mind. It is possible to do so, I assure you. They are always deviling and fooling someone - tho they pretend to try to keep the secret. This secret must not be kept from general technicals - they must know as much as possible about the apparatus, for just to see it operate explains a lot about energy one could not know before. I think this attraction of tech mind to the antique apparatus and its nature can be done left-handedly in some manner - figure on it. Some stories definitely contain a great knowledge of this apparatus - but does it reach the men it should?

Remember Mr. Rap, I don't expect you to tilt with this windmill in any way, I am only making sure you understand its existence - the facts of the thing - and how unbelievable their stupidity is - for tho they hold under their ray great sections of earth, they make no attempt to rule openly or to recruit such men as Coolidge and other physicists to bring out the value of the old mech, but go on as if it was still a medieval world - still hide and gibber or fail (when well intended) to bring order out of the chaos that is ray.

I am partly trying to warn you of the danger in them and I feel an impulse to make sure you understand that they do still exist and always did - the real source of the magic myths. - Richard Sharpe Shaver, Barto, Pennsylvania.

Dear Mr. Palmer:
Yesterday I received your circular regarding the next four issues of "The Hidden World", and as I have wanted for some time to write you personally, this has given me the prod to do it. I only hope you will find time to read this, and let me have your personal answer, if at all possible.

First, I have only the first four books, which I ordered

last April, according to my records. I have not renewed for the next four, nor even read all of those I have; and the reason is, I have been literally afraid to read them! There were a couple of strange "coincidences", which may have been nothing more than that, of course. But the very first evening I sat down to read, the lights in my living-room began flickering, dimming and then brightening, giving me a very eerie feeling. Then the effect of these tales of unspeakable cruelty and horror in those underground caves was so unpleasant, that I felt it was bad for me to fill my mind with such images, whether they were "true" or not. So I placed the whole stack on the floor underneath a little end-table in my closet-dressing-room, where my telephone is. Some two or three weeks later I removed the scarf which covered this table, in order to dust it - and was surprised to find that across the dark wood was a zig-zag, wavy line, which I had never seen there before, in a lighter tone than the rest. It looks something like this, on a larger scale

When I told my daughter about this, as she shares my interest in the strange and mysterious, to some degree, she assured me that this mark must have been there all the time, and that it was ridiculous for me to connect it with the books underneath it. But it does seem strange that I had never noticed that wavy line before, since I'd had that little table for years! Tho how such inanimate objects as books could do this, is another mystery!

Let me say that I do not for a moment think that Shaver was just perpretrating a hoax, and I do not question his sincerity. He had an experience of some sort, however you interpret it. But was it an objective one, or purely subjective? I hope it was the latter. Did all this arise from his subconscious mind, some split-off part of his personality? Or did he travel in his "astral body" to these caverns, as seems quite possible? I should very much like to know whether he actually made his escape from this prison? His account is reminiscent of the apostle Paul's rescue from prison, with the help of an "angel".

It seems to me that you could, and should, find out

1788

whether he was missed. (Perhaps you have by this time.) It would throw a great deal more light on the whole problem. And what would this sleep-walking guard have to say, the one who let him out?

It strikes me that there are a great many internal inconsistencies in his narrative. If he entered the caves by a door, however disguised, it seems he would be able to guide others to this entrance. He should know the approximate location at least. And if there is a way in, there is a way out, so why shouldn't the good tero come up here, and escape the awful persecutions of the dero? And what do the population down there subsist on, since there can't be any agriculture, nor the raising of flocks, nothing to produce food? Even if they do occasionally get a meal from goods stolen from the surface, or upon disappearing persons, surely those disappearances are not frequent enough, or upon a large enough scale, to feed all these underground people.

Again, if our ancient forebears did flee this planet, why did they leave behind such valuable mechanisms; why wouldn't they have taken these things with them when they left? Their flight couldn't have been so precipitate as all that, since we have survived these many centuries under this same poisonous sun. And this theory about our sun reverses everything I have ever thought, that the sun is the very source of life as we know it, and without the light, heat and energy of the sun, no life could exist. It is photosynthesis that is the basis of plant life, which nourishes the animals, and thence man. Even if we admit, as we do, that there are certain harmful rays emanating from the sun, (from which we are mostly screened), I have always thought of sunshine as being necessary to life and well-being, and certainly to our happiness. I might understand men seeking a "new" sun, but that anyone should deliberately seek to dwell in the dark, (and then proceed to manufacture light and heat artificially), is beyond belief. Especially to migrate to a sunless planet, where the cold must be beyond our imagination!

I'll concede that I was impressed by Shaver's apparently marvellous knowledge of scientific facts, and his mechanical

1789

knowledge, altho I know nothing much of such things. Or is it only pseudo-scientific? I don't know how he got all of it, and how authentic it is, but some of it seems to ring true. But his terms, "mech", and so many others, remind me of the slang of our "underworld", and I was not impressed by his Mantong alphabet, for some reason. How is it that these underground people use the English slang terms so freely, since they have lived for centuries apart from us? Even on the surface, we have very distinct languages. (I'm having a hard time just now, trying to learn French.) Even old English would be pretty unintelligible to the most of us. He would probably explain that they pick it up by telepathy, but how can they if they are so stupid?

I certainly do believe in telepathy, ESP, and all the rest of it, and have taken these things for granted all my life. But to believe that it can all be accounted for mechanically, and it is done by machines, is something I rather doubt. If such an apparatus as "Telaug" exists, or these contrivances that project apparitions and illusions - well, I'd have to be convinced. Or at least be convinced that such degraded specimens would know how to operate them and keep them in working order at all, even for their base purposes.

Another theory I've had all my life, you've blasted to bits. And that is, that evil is self-destructive, and no such mad society could long survive. Altho I'm not a particularly religious person, I have believed that a beneficent providence would put an end to evil when it got just too bad. It is hard to understand, when you read of some terrible fire, in which children are burned to death, etc., but at least one has the consolation of knowing that they found their release in death. Here, in Shaver's books, we have these fiends keeping their helpless victims living thoughout unspeakable torture, even so long as twenty years! And I had always believed that when pain became truly unbearable, nature would step in and bring the blessed relief of death. What a blow to faith that is, and the question, "Why doesn't God do something about it?" becomes more insistent. Oh yes, I've very often felt, too, that after the Creator made this world and established laws, he just went away and left it to run itself, just

1790

as Shaver thinks. But what do any of us know for sure? About anything?

Another thought I had, if these dero are so devoid of any human feeling, how could they bring up any children, or how could any of them survive? If there were such beings, they should long ago have depopulated themselves, if they are really human and not just astral devils.

You made a statement in one of your editorial comments, that you had seen a ghost, and you had also seen a dero. I should like to have you amplify on that, where and under what circumstances you did see a dero. I, too, have seen a ghost, at least once; in fact I grew up in a haunted house, tho I never learned by whom or why it was haunted. I have also seen a flying saucer, in the fall of 1946, about a year before anyone heard of them, and before the term "flying saucer" had even been coined. Yes, I have even heard voices, tho not of the sort Mr. Shaver heard, and that you heard when you visited him in Pennsylvania. I know what I have seen and heard because they were my experiences. And I have had some horrible dreams that could not possibly have been the product of my own mind (I hope). But none of this proves the existence of a dero, which I have never seen, to my knowledge. I think possibly I am a "sensitive", which is certainly no great advantage to me. And tho I believe somewhat in the claims of spiritualism, I have never attended a seance, for the same old reason, that I am afraid to.

It seems to me that Mr. Shaver does show some signs of paranoia in his ranting and raving at society in general for not taking him more seriously, when he has presented nothing to back up his theories, at least nothing that can be considered solid proof. But he has told us at the outset that we are helpless in the grip of these forces anyway - that we have no weapons against those rays, and so forth. Just what does he propose? Surely they don't have the atom bomb down there, and it seems a good place for one if all he says is true. The further I read, the more I suspect that his great hankering for these wonderful machines is a stronger motive than rescuing the victims of the awful cruelties he describes,

1791

which would be my first motive. And isn't the possession of the "stim" machines the uppermost consideration? Since there is so much sexuality, as well as brutality, in these stories, I wonder if we could get a clue there?

Now, since it was during your visit to Mr. Shaver in Pennsylvania that you heard the voices too, it must have been thru him as an instrument that you were able to hear them. For I assume you did not hear these voices on other occasions. I do not mean to infer that he was directly responsible, by no means, but that they in some way came thru him. By the way, I wonder if it was actually during Shaver's employment as a welder that this sort of thing thing began, or was that a part of the fictionalizing?

I am still not able to bring myself to wade thru all these stories in their entirety, but have skimmed, reading mostly footnotes, letters and comments. One thing that seems inconsistent is that his estimate of the numbers of the wicked dero and their evil natures, seems to be modified as you go along. Later on they don't outnumber the tero so overwhelmingly, and don't seem quite so inhuman as they did in the first of the stories! But you have now promised us the "Real Thing", and I am cautious as to whether I can take it or not. If the first four volumes are "sugar-coated", what a bitter pill the real truth must be! Of course, since I did not renew, and haven't the second four books, there may be a lot I have missed which might answer some of my questions. Or was it just more of the same?

I might put forth a hesitative or tentative theory in regard to Dick Shaver. Altho you said you were sure he was not unbalanced, and was of sound mind, yet I cannot help remembering that later you wrote that he was ill and unable to write. Now I consider that I am of sound mind too, (I must be, as I have held some responsible jobs for years) yet, at one time, over thirty years ago, I suffered what was euphemistically called a "nervous breakdown". While I can hardly bear to recall what I went thru then, I do know that never in my life was my mind so incredibly fertile, active and creative! Millions of wonderful ideas rushed thru my brain, and they were perfectly logical, too. I was never more logical in my life. Mainly, I was occupied in trying to piece together a complete theory of cosmogony, a synthesis of all I had ever read, mainly based on mythology. It seemed pretty impressive, and at one time I declared that I knew "everything"! But at last it all crashed of its own weight, and I don't know anything at all. Could this have a bearing, I wonder?

However, I hasten to add, it was not during this period of my life that I had "psychic" experiences, but during times of perfect health. While I was so ill, I saw nothing and heard nothing out of the ordinary; it was all going on in my own mind, not outside. Yet I did have many unexplainable experiences, mostly as a young person, which I have not submitted to any publication, altho I have sometimes thought of writing about them to Fate Magazine, for instance, to which I have subscribed almost from the first.

My main interests are not in "pulps", but in "high-brow" magazines, the Atlantic, Horizon, etc., to name a few. The only reason that I ever dabbled in these far-out things is that I seemed to be drawn to them thru my own early experiences. And this is not very reasonable, since the whole subject was so terrifying to me, and I used to lie in a cold sweat of fear many a night in the old house where I grew up. I suppose it is kind of perverse fascination.

Now to identify myself somewhat, I work for Leo Burnett Advertising Co., Inc., in the Accounting Department, and I do the billing and paying in the magazines. Can you imagine a more humdrum, prosaic job? So at least I am not just a crack-pot, and I do have a background of some education. As to my private life, am a widow in my sixties (alas), brought up four children alone, and still have to work for a living. I live alone – something I used to think I'd be afraid to do, but am never afraid here, and I want to keep it that way, you see?

I didn't really mean to write such a long letter, and I realize I have asked a great many questions. If you could find time to answer some of them, I would greatly appreciate it. Then I might consider whether to renew my subscription of not. It isn't just a question of the money involved, and I should really like to see you succeed in your venture. I hope I am not asking too much. - Mrs. Bernice R. Knapp, 520 W. Cornelia Ave., Apt. #211, Chicago 13, Illinois.

Dear Sir:
Since you were so interested in the antique language I sent you in hopes it would so reach intelligent minds and not be lost again to man, I venture to write you about it and kindred matters. Nothing pleased me more than the fact that you even partially understood it, for to preserve the thing for man has been a burden I have borne for long alone. The language is important for much more practical reasons than the usual studies of antiquity, for they were a scientific race, perhaps the very one whose existence gave rise to the God legends which we all think of as complete fairy tales, but which were not in truth anything but the remnants of the race memory of great beings which once existed on earth.

Now the language - if you study it as I have done for years - gives one many illuminating insights into their much greater knowledge of the nature of energy and matter. For instance: their concept of matter as integrative is obviously much more correct than ours of matter as still - static - dead. Obviously it is growing - for something flows into it all the time as the force of gravity. That they handled this force of integration and made beneficial vibrants of its food - the exdisintegrance or energy ash - is shown by many of their expressions. Perhaps the most important message we get from them is their knowledge of de as a force that distorts thought into detrimental will - thus their word dero as one who is robot to disintegrant energy is an explanation of our villains and our Hitlers, because knowing the cause of detrimental will is the first step toward decreasing the trouble on earth - obviously there would be little trouble if there were no detrimental will.

I wish you would let me see your notes made on the language and then I could more easily give you my views and explanations so that it would be more clear to you what a tremendous lead on the problems our physicists face this

1794

thing can be - but to get them to see it has been my problem - few of them could ever believe there was wisdom in the past long enough to give serious thought to the language you can understand.

I have written a couple of stories containing some of my ideas about the language and what it gives us - but only sent them once and doubt they were read - as most of the scientifiction mags are not even reading new material now I gather. Nevertheless will send them again hoping you will look at them, since you showed such intelligent interest in my language.

Another thing one gleans from the language is the cause of age - which they knew was due to sun-thrown radio-actives - and which they guarded against in the same way that the grass guards its seed from age, tho dying itself. The grass retains the poison in its stem - and the seed keeps its fresh power of growth uncontaminated. This function of the plant stem and the placenta of the womb they duplicated by filters and centrifuges for their own intake of liquids and the seeds and nuts and fruits are themselves fairly clean of age, as are also new-born animals. Our medicoes and technicians have no rational explanation for age or the difference between old and young tissue, but they (the ancients) knew and used the knowledge to give rise to the legend of the immortal Gods. There is nothing more fascinating or stimulating to the imagination than ferreting out their words and deducing the information they contain; for the sake of the future, DO NOT DROP THE ANTIQUE ALPHABET. KEEP ON WITH IT! There is another antique language of the same time - the language of opposites. It is keyed by the word LIVE - spelled backward it is EVIL - there are any number of these words which have a directly opposite meaning - such as PIT and TIP and which also all spell each other when reversed - but I get no tips on physics from it. It is probably a less direct ancestor of English.

Now, my intelligent editor, it is very difficult to sum all this up for you in a single letter. Will you therefore write me what you gathered of it and I will have a way of filling

1795

the missing spaces and giving you the work I have done on it - little of which is written but nevertheless exists, tho only in my mind. It must not stay there unread by perhaps more able men. We must take care of this thing. I have a theory that once a book existed called The T book, which was rather widespread and in use down till Christ's time as a book which contained the elemental frames of logic and simple what-to-dos like the age poison solution of theirs which is not at all complicated in concept. But some group feared the T book and destroyed it completely - so that only the memory of that once infallible book remains - and which memory was the father of the bible and all its veneration including the cross on the cover - but one mustn't mention such theories today, even today the religious fly off the handle at the idea that the bible is not the bible but a substitute book put out to keep the people dumb sometime in the past. Well, such thoughts are not concrete like the alphabet - thank God its parts are still alive in the sound meanings of everyday speech. There is a great deal more to be got from it than ever I got, and that was amazing enough to suit the most exacting fan you have. You see, "de" can be struggled with and guarded against in the laboratory once it is recognized, and "exd" - the food of all integrance - (corresponds to our concept of ether) can be isolated in a vibrant - a ray - which is beneficial to health and increasing to growth - by simple test of magnetic field screens and living cell battery copies (colpoids) but no one is pointed in that direction. The concept of beneficial force as a possible thing - as the real direct lead toward a greater future for man - needs strengthening for the general mind has no aim toward growing a better brain - and no progress is truly progress unless man grows a better brain to grow a better brain with. The pattern of progress is that - to grow a growth to grow a growth to grow etc., yet even that fact is unrecognized so far as I know. That is one reason their language is hard to grasp at first - our concepts are finite while they knew the growth concept. We have the concept of cessation ingrained - they did not recognize it except as a

1796

manifestation of de force. I think that many of their words were followed by a little sign meaning much what our letter n (to the n'th power) means in math. But the very concept of continuing growth is lost as well as the symbol. I think what men need most is a more conscious aim toward a more desirable goal - toward the knowledge of man growth, in truth. They do not have a conscious aim toward a more desirable goal - toward the knowledge of man growth, in truth. They do not have a conscious aim toward a desirable goal that will stand analyzing, to my mind. To learn how to grow into a man better able to grow into a wiser man is a goal followed by but a few men out of all the number who could be striving in that direction. They called such a goal "TIC" and any energy which was not directed toward that goal they called "ERR". Alexis Carrel says much the same thing, as you can tell by the title of his book "MAN THE UNKNOWN". He is one of the few men on earth whose efforts are not err to self interest - that is, he aims to understand his life process and make it last longer. True self interest is seen in his efforts and in very few others. They think of self interest as an oppositional of other self interests - which is a de illusion (their disillusion) for oppositionals neutralize. True self interest would thus be a coincident always - never an oppositional. Thus our most basic concepts have become err from disintegrant force distortion of thought flows over the long periods of time since we were the children of the Gods of the past. I would very much like to get some of their thought again resurrected into the general mind - I have a great deal to unburden myself of and know no other field but scientifiction to use for the purpose.

I have read Amazing Stories since the first issue under Gernsback, and God love him for what he did to youth's thought. Knowing that you too have a mind, since you really grasped that there was something to my antique alphabet, I have hopes for the future of the magazine. I liked his policy of insisting that there be some real base in science fact for a story no matter how it be developed - for his authors did put ou some awakening thought. Somehow, some writers just don't grasp this need for caring for the young concept, and one worries, tho perhaps needlessly. I answered a couple of dozen letters inquiring for more details on the language. Wait till they work with it awhile, I'll really be busy. - Richard Sharpe Shaver, Barto, Pennsylvania.

SEEING IN THE "DARK"

By R. B. Hoag, M.D.

I WAS in a depressed state of mind in that life. For years things had not been satisfying in our Clan. We had been forced to take a number of men from other Clans into ours, to be part of it. They had been trained in an other Clan. We were a small Clan, so that the men who had come from other Clans were a disturbing social force. Not that there was any opposition; it was not that. What I am trying to explain is that there were clan-differences. A man has to be born into a Clan, grow up in it, to know how to adjust to that Clan. (With women these differences are the expected thing. It is normal to marry into another Clan. In ancient times for men to change Clans was unusual.) The men who had joined with us were fine. They wanted to be true members of the Clan. They gave themselves to us in a fine way. I do not want to give a wrong impression about those fine men. When all are not born in the Clan, the problems that arise are difficult. If one man of a party was from a "foreign" Clan, others of the party would feel that he did not understand us as well as our own ones would. We were always feeling that we had to be on the watch, lest we be discourteous to one who had come from some other Clan.

I had not been myself for some days. My foot, that I had got a piece of a cactus-needle deep into, had a way of being troublesome at times. Now was one of those times. For a long period I had done no work away from home. It was in my mind that, maybe, I was to know why I had to stay near home, those days; maybe some purpose was in that.

In my two hands, that time, were the many strands of fine flexible roots. I was trying to work out a new design. My mind was being lulled by doing work at that pretty hand-weaving. It was like a game with me. I did that when my mind needed to be in passive feeling. It had done me good, at times, to do that work. I had just seen that the two small girls who had been on a visit to my wife, at our home, were taking their departure, to go to their own home. We had some of the homes of our scattered settlement down in great queer grooves that floods had cut far into the rock, near the bottom of the small gorge our good stream of water was in. Our place of our settlement, our pagus, was far out in a bad desert. It was a strange good place, far out in a wide extensive dry desert. The stream we had was one that lost itself in the desert, not very far from where our settlement was. I will tell no more about that now. You need to know that those two small Indian girls were going along on the smooth bare rock of the big groove of the gorge. They were twins. You would not know which one of them it was. They were in some kind of a game. They were walking backward, one a little in front of the other one. Each one had hold of a short small-rope. They were saying together words of their game.

How good we felt, when they would come to do us a visit. My wife was one who knew well how to do with children. How we both liked young children. (By that time our own children had gone from us; they were grown, so that they had families of their own.)

I saw how they were doing, I was liking the pretty picture of that. They were pretty girls. They were in good fine Indian pretty colored mantles, dressed up special for going

1800

to visit in the home of their friend (my wife). Their mother and my wife were friends, of course. We were not neighbors near to that other family; it was a considerable way the little girls would have to go to get to their home.

I saw movement beyond the two girls. The small dog, a young thing (the dog the girls had brought there with them), had come back; (he had gone on ahead). I saw that he was afraid. I knew by that something unusual was on the way, around the bend of the gorge. I was, then, knowing that some stranger had come. I got to my feet. I was in some disturbance in my mind lest the two small girls be frightened. I went toward them, making talk, so as to keep them looking my way, not to look behind them to see the small dog that had come back; they had not seen that their dog had come back. I got to the girls, went past them, and soon saw a young, tall stranger-Indian.

Immediately I knew him. He had grown some since I had seen him years before, in his own settlement, but I knew him. He was sad; I saw that he had gone through some great personal sorrow. I went to him. I felt how things were with him. He was all in sorrow when he knew that I felt how things were with him. I had no need to ask him what it was. The fact that he was there, very far from his own settlement, and was deeply sad, made me know that his wife had died. He was young for such a thing to happen to him. (He was the young Minstrel of the big Clan from which some of the young men had come to live with us in our Clan, as husbands of some of our young women.) I saw how deep his grief was. He had come to me. I was in deep feeling, when I knew that he had felt that I, rather than some friend of his own Clan, was the one who could help him in this bad time of his life.

We, my wife and I, were then in the time of life when we were thinking that we needed to get to doing some special work. Our work with our children had been finished. They, our children, had their homes not in our own Clan, but in that Clan from which this young Minstrel had come. (Except my one son; he had him home in our settlement.) We were thinking that we would have to migrate from our Clan. Our

1801

clan-work was finished. Young men were doing the work that I had done. It is not a good thing for the young man who takes over your work to have you be there in the Clan. In some cases some of my old friends would still come to me, instead of to the young Chief of the Scouts. I had turned that work over to the big son of the Chief. He was good at that. Of course it was not good to have two Chief-Scouts in the Clan. Then, there was the matter of the work of minstrel. I had had that work to do too. I had given that work up to a young Indian. He, that young Indian, was feeling that he was not at all the right one to do that work. I will not tell more of that here. I needed to have you be, in a small way, in on how things were with us, my wife and I, at that time.

We stood there, that stranger Indian and I, looking down into the clear water of the stream (some five hands below the smooth rock-floor on which we stood). He was not then in good strength. I saw that he had gone the very long journey from his settlement to ours without having the good care about his eating that he should have had. I was in the feeling that my wife would take care of that. They had had no living children. A bad sad thing had happened. Each time the baby had died, before it had been born. The last time, the mother was too weak to go on living. They had been in great grief, because they had had no children. He knew that some deep thing was wrong, or that bad thing would not have happened. His wife, before she had died, had shown her husband that he should be one in my home, should go to me. (We, the young Minstrel and I, were close friends, near friends in the Long-life of us. His wife knew that.) I tell you these things, for you need to know, here at the beginning of the story, things that were in the minds of the ones of the story, at that time. That was very long ago. It was in a region now known as part of desert Arizona. I was an Indian in North America for a very long time many cycles of my life, far back in ancient time. (I use the name "Indian", for it is the best name we now have for the wild persons who preceded the more tame people who came in the later eras.)

As I looked down into the clear of the water, it came to me to ask him how the thing was that had been bothering

1802

him, when I was there, a number of years before that time. (He had not wanted to be the Minstrel.) Another Indian had been trying to get to be chosen as Minstrel.

"He was killed," my friend said. "The man who is now Minstrel is a good one. My own doing of that work could not be good, for I am too young a man. I did what I could do for a while after you went away. Then, the man who was the proper one for that was found by the Chief. Of course I was glad. I had not ever done anything before the Clan. My way was to go try to get some old person to be Minstrel. When I had found that the poor old man who had shown me my deep things was in much deeper things that I had known about, I went to the Chief, and told him. That got the Chief to talk that old man into being the Minstrel. I went from my Clan with no obligation to the Clan on me. I will not go back there. I feel that there is a place far in the north where I must go. I seem to know that I have work to do, far there. It may be that I can find my way to that place."

My foot was paining me all the time, those days. You know how it is with pain; it will not let you forget that it is there. I have put all this here in the beginning of my book. You will wonder why. I need to get you into the story I am to tell you. I have things to tell you, by means of a long story. You need to know something about how things were, before you can go along with the story in an understanding way. Pain - what is that? I am one who "wonders". "Wonder" is very important to deep thinking. If you are to get good help from the reading of this book, you must do wondering. How bad it is that the whole human race is complacent, this era of its long history. You cannot but feel that the human race thinks that it has now "come of age", so that it "knows its way about in the world". It is now worse off than it ever was before. The worst calamity that every happened to the human race is happening now. I do not mean the outer things, all the terrible war-things. How terrible all that is. But, the meaning, the significance, of all that; that is what is the actual calamity. If the great intelligent human race cannot get along together in some kind of peaceable way, after all the many centuries of trying something deeply wrong must

1803

be the cause. That hidden cause of all the terrible HELL we are all down in - the blindness of practically all human persons to the significance of that titanic thing is what I mean by the greatest calamity that has happened to the human race in all time. We have gone further down than ever before into the darkness of the "dark-ages". It is a fact that the whole human race is still in the "dark ages". (What makes an age be one of the "dark ages" is not any absence of light, not darkness; it is blindness of the deep mind.) More blind than ever before are the many millions of people of the human race. That is the very terrible calamity.

I need to get you to wondering. I need to get you to knowing that complacency is one of the worst forms of blindness. The human people are not at all as wise as they were very far back in ancient times. They do not even know that they are living the Long-life. They do not know about the deep mind each person has. All the grand expensive "education" of the people everywhere is merely for training the less-deep mind, the reasoning-mind. People believe that everything has to be reasoned out. They seem to get no feeling that the great terrible cumulation of "Big-Business" bad management that now is devastating whole countries, many of them, is a titanic reductio ad absurdum of the idea that with the reasoning minds of people things can be worked out to the satisfaction of everybody. The deep cause of the whole age-old HELL is not even dreamed of - use of the less-deep mind for telling things that can be told only by the deep mind.

I was thinking that it would be good, right here, to do something to get you to feel how things have to be worked out by the deep mind, if they are subtle things, or complicated things. It is not enough merely to say that the reasoning-mind cannot do that kind of work. You need to feel that - and go wondering, as you do your things, day after day after day.

It is a small story that I will tell you. "Do not be in any haste to do anything about that," my father said. I was very angry. It was a thing that was very terrible; I had seen

1804

what had been done. I had just seen a small boy killed. It was not accident. A mad woman, the boy's mother, had done that. I was yet young, that cycle of my life. I thought that the Chief should go there and kill the woman. He, my father, was not at all one to be mild about anything that was bad. This was different. It was a big bad complicated thing. To kill the woman - there was the whole bad matter of a possible feud. One family is, as it were, a small Clan within the big Clan. That thing the mad mother had done was an extreme case of what many mothers did. All the families needed to take that thing to heart. Then, killing the bad person is, in some cases, too easy on that one who did the bad thing. I was not in any liking of what my father said: "Go far away from the settlement. You are in no condition now to say a word about that thing. You are too hot in your heart. Go keep vigil."

Though I did not want to do that; I went. It was the very thing. My friend, my wise father, went to the poor distracted mother. He told her he knew just how terrible on her that was. He said that he knew that she had had no intention to do that to her boy. He talked to her, in a kind understanding way. He saw that the woman had not been right in her mind when she had done that.

He took her into his own home. She lived a sheltered life in our home several years. She, little by little, got so she could go out in the settlement and mingle with her friends of the times before that thing had happened. Of course it made a great difference in her life. She was low in her mind, so that she did only hidden work for the other families. Of course that thing had broken up her own home.

I have told you this story to show you that all that could not have been worked out by the less-deep mind of any person, or persons. My father had good use of his deep mind. He felt what was the right thing to do. The thing was taken care of in the best possible way. Had my plan been followed, a bad division of the Clan would have come. Wars have been started by such things as that.

In the long-ago times all human persons had better use of the deep mind than most persons have now, in this

1805

era of human history. All down the ages the ability to use the deep mind has been gradually leaking away. It is that loss of the ability to use the deeper purer mind, that constitutes the terrible titanic calamity that now is cursing the whole human race to worse wars, after bad ones, and to worse anguish. Why do millions of people like to read a book like "Forever Amber"? Competent reviewers have said that the big book is crudely bawdy, not any of it literature. Yet, it is a "great success". The movie rights to use that have been sold for many thousands of dollars. The earth-wide powerful rich Macmillan book publishing company have gone down, - since the time when they published the book "Maria Chapdelaine", and the good potent "Modern Reader's Bible". At the time when the whole human race is in the worst psychologic calamity it was ever in, they put that end of a book out. If that be not evidence of blindness of the deep mind, what is it? Are there not already millions enough of "sexy" people in the earth, that millions more of them should be grown? Has a rich book-publishing company no obligation and responsibility? How much that company could have done, in these times, to make "best sellers" of deep-going books.

One more thing, and I will go to the story. In these times only the publishers of books can get books out to the people. It is the accepted custom for the millions of readers of books to get their books from the companies that publish books to make money. No other purpose than that have they. How very difficult it is for a poor unknown thinker to get his book even read by any big publisher of books. That condition of affairs constitutes an impassible "road-block" between the millions of people of the whole human race and the deep thinkers, ones who alone are able to show the way up out of the HELL we are all in.

Ki-Mo-Go was the name of that young Indian. He had got to know me years before that time. I had gone the long way to the big Clan he was a member of. He and I had been intimate then. I had lived in his home, those months. He and I had much in common. We had got to know that, in a former cycle of our lives, we had been brothers. So,

1806

he was like one of the family when he had come to us and was in our home.

In two short things I will get you to knowing some things you need to know. Ki-Mo-Go was not in the lodge, the next morning. He had gone away in the night. His pack was gone. We felt that he had had to go away without waiting for morning to come. Being a Minstrel, I knew that he had gone to do something great invisible Ko-Waa wanted him to do. He was away seven hands of days. He had been down in deep-vastation. He had gone the far way to the rim of the great deep strange canyon. We got to know about all that. He had lived many years, the preceding cycle of his life, in a small lodge down a short way below the top of the cliff of the great canyon, at a place where the noise of the high falls, down in the bottom of the deep canyon, could be heard, if the wind was right. He had, as he said, kept vigil for years in that place. A terrible thing had happened to him, earlier, that "yesterday" cycle of his life. He had been the only person who had escaped death in one of those terrible raids by a base war-party. He alone was left alive. Under dead bodies, the one living Indian was not known to be still alive. He had had to "live with that" all the remaining years of that "yesterday" cycle of his life. Young Ki-Mo-Go had got much back from his experience alone, as a deep thinker, the preceding cycle of the "long-life" of him. I will get you to knowing something about that, by telling you a story Ki-Mo-Go told us, my wife and me. I like to do my things with stories.

"I was not liking to go on living," young Ki-Mo-Go said. "At that time, the 'yesterday' cycle, I was old and worn and thin from not doing my eating regularly. I had got into not-good ways in my living. My former ways had been strict. My old friends, two old goats, had been killed. I was in bad feeling from the loss of their good friending with me. I was down, in my mind. Good great invisible Ko-Waa does not be enough. You do the best you can with that friending with the invisible friend. But you need more than that. You are in need of at least some animal-friends. I was doing more sleeping than was good for me. I had got

1807

listless. I was wishing that I would die. It would not be good to go out that way. I wanted to go out a quick way. One evening it came to me that I might try to go yet again all the long dangerous hard way down to the great falls. So, I put that up to Ko-Waa. Early the next morning, first thing, when I had come up out of sleep, the noise of faraway great Falls came to my ears, very clear. Of course I knew that was invisible great Ko-Waa, telling me that I should make that attempt. Years had passed, since I had gone down into the great canyon. The way down was not at all an easy one. I had to use my long-rope more times than I liked. My rope was old. But, why should I not fall, and go out quickly? Better anyway to be doing something, than to stay on in that stale disagreeable lone life, there where everything spoke to me of my two old friendly goats. They could almost talk. They knew me, and I knew them. I had the feeling that their going down into the death-sleep was the sign that I too would soon be doing that.

"I took my time. It was, I think, one hand of days before I got to the last cliff. I was not nearly as bad in my mind by that time as I had been when I had started down. It is good to be working at some dangerous thing. I knew that my rope was not good, in one place, not far from one end of it. So, I let that bad end of my long hair-rope be the bottom end of it. I got down to the place where the weak part of the rope was. I was tired. I was lonely. I had got nearly all the way down to the bottom of the deep canyon. 'Why do I not let this be the end of me?', that thought came into my mind. I had only a little food with me. It is bad, if you have to starve. Getting to death that way is not good. I went slowly on past that weak place. Unless the great ONE would tell me to do it, I would not kill myself. But no harm in hoping that the rope would break. I waited and stopped there, thinking that the hairs might give way a little, and then the rope might break. I went on down slowly. Near the end of the rope it happened; the rope broke. I fell. It was not far. I was lamed in my foot. I went, limping, on down, the piece of rope in my hand. I saw myself, as I was doing that. It came to me that it was a sign. A sign that I was near to the end of that cycle of my life."

That story Ki-Mo-Go told not all at one time. We were at a cold time, in our gorge. We had a fire in the lodge, those nights. We were but three of us in the lodge. My wife had put up some blankets for curtains, so that our friend had part of the lodge as his own. It was good. We felt that Ki-Mo-Go was a son. We liked the feeling of again having a big boy in our home. We burned pine cones to get the nuts from them. As we did that, Ki-Mo-Go would tell some of his story. We were with good interest in life again, my wife and I. You know how it is when your children all go from your home. Now, we had us another son. He was not like our own son. Ki-Mo-Go was more like I was; he liked to work around home. He was good at woodwork. He showed me some things about woodwork, at the time when I was in the home of his father, that I had not known before. He had shown me how to make a wheel. (They used wheels to get water up out of wells, in that big Clan, well-wheels.)

"I got down to the river," Ki-Mo-Go said, resuming the story. "I was not thinking that I was in any condition to try to get down to the place of the great falls, for my foot was in pain. I was wondering what the sign of that pain was. Of course everything unusual that happened to me was some kind of a sign to me, given to me by invisible Ko-Waa. I had got so I was not ever thinking of the great invisible Mother, Mo-Kaa. So long had I been away from women, that I had not been right in my friending with the invisible Mother. It was so, with me, that I would talk out loud to the great Father: 'What do you mean by this pain?' The answer came: 'You were trying to let yourself fall.' (That came to me, as the answer to my question.) 'That falling on rocks is not a good way to die.' I had my answer. I had got so I did not mind the pain. I went on down the considerable distance I had to go to get to the place, above the falls, where, years before that time, I had camped. A small side-stream came down there. I was not ever liking the sad thing the great deep canyon stood for. Of course we Indians all knew well the terrible great sign that was. It was a thing that would be there forever, as a big sign to all

1809

human peoples. I was not liking it that it was there, down in that great wound in Mother-Ground, that I would go down into the death-sleep. Of course I knew that cycle of my life was a not-normal one.

"In the night I came up out of sleep to find that Moon was looking down on me. Moon and I were good friends. 'What is it, Daa-Kai-Lai?' I asked, saying my words out loud. He did a strange thing. He was not in any clear shining, for mist was there, in the place of the great river, so that I saw Moon with the glow of his coming to me through the mist. He, Moon, went entirely from my sight. With that, he answered my question. 'So that is it,' I said. 'I am to have my light go out.' I was glad. It is good to know that thing. Moon had done me many a good turn in all the lone years of my long vigil. (How good it is to have some of the Sky-ones as your good deep-knowing friends.) I knew that that was the last night I would see my friend, Moon. I got up. I was in my feeling good that my end would come that soon. 'I will go me now to do my honor to the great Faller-down-of-much water". He would not like it, if I had come the long way down to visit him and I had gone to sleep before I had got all the way to him. I was not thinking much about how I was to go to my death; that was in the hands of the great invisible Father. I was very tired with living my lone life. I had thought out my troubles, so that I saw my way clearly through all of them. I knew that my work was finished, that cycle of my life. In a small thought that came to me, as I was limping my way slowly along, it came to me that it was a deep kind of a way to do to seem not to care at all what came, that night. 'If you like,' I said in my mind to great Ko-Waa, 'you can have me slip, and fall into the great falls.'

"When I got to the place from which I would look at the grand thing, a little beyond the place where the great river suddenly decides to take a much lower road, I was feeling pleased. My friend, good Moon, had been there before me, to do a strange mystery-thing. I wouldn't wonder but he had got many of the Little-people to help him with that. It was the thing to make it seem that there was hardly any drop to

1810

death at all, just a going down a little way, and getting into something like the finest soft down-feathers of a great mother goose. I was in delight. In the deep gorge downstream from the great falls there was Moon-mist, a long deep lake of that very soft stuff. Even the noise of the high falls seemed to be hushed some. I saw; I understood: Moon was giving me a picture of going down into the death-sleep. It would not be the terrible fall. The great falls, as they had been, were not the picture of my going down into the deep sleep. Moon had fixed things up so that I would know that death would be an easy one.

"I did my honor to mighty massive loud-talking Falls. Of course when you talk to such a one as he is, you have to use all the force in your voice you have. I yelled out as loud as I could to him. He saw me. (He may have forgotten about me, I thought, for it has been years since I was here.) He laughed. It was funny: thin old Indian yelling out some words to him. I liked the noise of his big laugh. I was glad when I knew he felt to laugh. He was, you might say, Death. Of course he knew how it was with me. With only half of one small look from out one of his many eyes he could see that I was ready to take the long jump. He was liking it that I was so good in my thinking about that, not solemn at all. My yell - it was a fine great happy one. He was, himself, like that. How he can take great jumps, and not mind it at all. He was saying to me things I needed to have in me, as I was about to go to my death. 'See,' great Falls seemed to say, 'I but go down to a lower trail; I stop not at all. Down there, I keep on going.'

"I fell into my sad serious way. My mind would go back, of course, at a time like that, to my mate, and to my children. Just then, a thing happened. I thought that it was some enemy-Indian, down there in the mist, a little below long massive level Pointing finger rock. Almost I let fly my arrow into him. He was near below me. I caught hold of myself. In a single fine wisp of time I knew him for what he was, a good father of a family. The thing I saw first was the black head of the Indian-boy, astride the neck of his big father. The woman was not far down, on the sliding

1811

slide-rock that they had toiled the long way up from out the bottom of the steep great gorge, there right at the falls. A small time the young Chief stopped, when he had seen what was above him, ominous long great black finger had thrust itself out through the rock to paint. The end of great level finger all but touched the rushing-down water of the mighty falls - at the thin place of the falls (the place I thought of as being a door into a great world of unknown ones). I had dreamed dreams, one time before, when I had camped some hands of days at that place.

"I soon knew that something bad was bothering those Indians. There were five of them, a family. Some enemy must have chased them there. I could feel the danger they were in. I had all my arrows. But, in the mist, what are arrows? I got me some throwing-stones. I did not let them see me. I got ready for the fight that I thought was to come. It came soon. Not any fight at all. How could I know what all that was? A bad old fat Indian showed up, on the slide-rock below the long finger of rock. The Indians were there on the finger, ready to throw rocks down. The big young man dropped a big rock down. I saw that he did that just to warn the old bad Indian. That one, I knew, was a very low base man. He did some things that made me know that. He was not in any feeling of good respect for the two women of that party. I was wondering what the sight of all that was. It came to me that all that had to do with things that were to come, when I had come up into my next cycle of life. That bad old fat Indian shot an arrow up. It brought blood. I shot him. He went down in death from my one sure arrow. But, mist was there. When the mist had cleared away, I was just in time to see a thing that brought my heart into my mouth; they all jumped into the falls. Splashes, and they were gone. How unreal everything seemed. But for the blood, and some throwing-stones on the long great finger of rock, all that might have been but some kind of a vision. I looked up to far Sky. How more than ever my loneliness came over me. A great homesickness came over me. I went back from the edge of the gorge. I took off my old things. I jumped to my death."

1812

What had got Ki-Mo-Go started to telling that story of Pointing-finger rock was the having in his hands an old bow, and the other things that went with it. I had told him the story of the finding of that old bow, below the place of the brink of the falls of the deep canyon. It had done the thing that had made him go off on that long journey, that time, start right off in the night, the first night he was at our home. He had come to know that that had been his bow, the "yesterday" cycle of his life. That it was, with the story I told of what had happened to our Chief at the great falls, that had made him go the long journey to the great canyon. He had gone into deep-vastation. He had got much back from the cycle of his life when he had lived the lone life, there at the great canyon, for many years.

We knew that we were to migrate from our Clan, my wife and I. It came to me that we would go with Ki-Mo-Go, and live with him, in a wild place far north of our region.

You who read this should feel that all this is a coming into the story, an introduction. I know that it would not do to take you into the story unprepared for it. It is a story that has in it things unusual, unusual in stories that persons write now, in these times. I need to go into some things, before I get started at the beginning of the story. In two small stories I will finish the introductory part of this book.

"Do not go," he said. "Your mother will need you here at the home. I must feel that some one is here with her." I was sad. I had thought that I would get the chance to go, that time. My older brother was the one, I thought, who should stay at home. He was the one who got all the chances to go with the Scouts when great things were done. In three days they brought my dead father and my dead brother home. How terrible that was. That cured me of the wanting to go fight enemies. I saw, it came over me, that all that fighting was like young boys, fighting. How bad much of the fighting among boys is. It does no good. It does not show who is right. It shows only who is the stronger, or the better in fighting, nothing more. That was many thousands of years ago. In all the time since that time I saw

1813

no reason to change my mind about that matter. That is one of my two stories. The other one from another cycle of my life, is this: "Do not take any more of his bad bragging. He will not do the right. He is spoiling for a fight. Go into it. You have showed him that you do not believe in fighting. You have been patient with all that long enough." I felt the same way that my mother did. I went out. He was there; (my mother had said that, because she had heard the voice of the bad big boy as he was coming near to our home). I fought him. That time, he got a great surprise. He had come to taunt me again. I wiped the ground with him. That ended that.

I opened the door on my story far along in it. I must now go back to the beginning of it, and take you along in it. I will have to write explanations sometimes, because of some bad conditions my story has to meet. I continually come up to something that makes it hard for me to go all out in my telling things. You can know that I have it hard from the fact that most people do not use the deep mind very much, but think that the way everybody should be doing is to "reason things out". The people of the whole earth are for "reasoning", planning things out. If you do not be beforehand with a "reasoned-out" plan, you are not a competent person, they think. That is the feeling everywhere. The President of our people has to try to "reason out" very many great complicated problems. Of course he has much help in that. But, how is he to know who the many helpers are, and what their ideas are? You know how that is. I am for going deep. If we had millions of persons like what the man Daniel was, long ago - there would be no terrible muss such as we have now. Of course once the millions of people are down in the muss, much reasoning is needed all the time. It is very complicated, the whole great thing. We must give good attention to the things that are happening, as we go along in our daily lives. I am doing writing-work. I cannot be all in that work, of course; I have to give some of my thinking to what is going on. In my kind of writing I can say out what I think, even if I have to stop my story to do that. It comes in right, so that I can do that.

1814

This morning I am beginning to do more of this book. My wife is near me, looking over an account of what our President said, in an important message to the great people he is the "Chief" of. We have talked some about that. We have not much time for these private talks, for she works out. We are not people who do not have to work. We would not like to think we were not doing anything to help out, in this terrible time. I am in hope that my writing can do some good. My wife is doing useful work. I have two married sons who are doing useful work. We are a working-family. I say these personal things to you - so that you may feel how we are. We should have good understanding between us, you who read this, and I who write. I would be glad to know you, whoever you are. If you are a foreigner, then all the more I would like to know you, for you could give me different ideas from what I am used to.

One small explanation is needed, before I begin the actual story. We are all friends. We are all members of the same great family, the great human family. I used to be having a good kind of a glow in my heart, when I was ancient-Indian, and would think of my own Clan. How good that was. With those glows in the hearts of all of us, our Clan was kept together, and was kept from misunderstandings. Now, though I have no Clan, I have that great Family. I can say to myself: "I am one of the great HUMAN family. I can feel my good glow in my heart because of that. I will say a thing: "Let our 'Chiefs' of our Nations try to hold all the people together with good wholesome glows in the hearts of them." How simple-minded millions of people will think that is. That, their being that way, is yet another thing that shows how blind in the deeper purer mind the millions of people are. It is blindness to many deep simple things that makes it hard for deep-thinkers to get people to listen to them. You see how it is; I write only my line, at that time. I do not "reason out" beforehand what I will do, in my writing-work. If I had not good use of my deep mind, so that it, and the great invisible friend, could do with me what needs to be done, how could I do this kind of work?

I have been having a feeling in my heart, as I have been

1815

writing. It is a thing that I like, a thing Robert Louis Stevenson wrote. I have been feeling a kind of a glow in my heart because of that. I will write out that thing. "There is an upright stock in a man's own heart that is trustier than any syllogism. And the eyes, and the sympathies and appetites know a thing or two that have never yet been stated in controversy. Reasons are as plentiful as blackberries; and, like fisticuffs, they serve impartially with all sides. Doctrines do not stand or fall by their proofs, and are only logical insofar as they are cleverly put. An able controversialist no more than an able general demonstrates the justness of his cause." In doing what you do use first your deep mind. The deep mind came first, in the Long-life of you. Put first things first. You could not have a reasoning mind at all, if you had not the deeper purer mind. This matter should be clear. You should know what the deep mind is, and what the less-deep mind is. You need clearness about this very important matter. If I should only say out to you my findings about that, you would get no deep good from it. I find that I will have to tell you a short story, so as to make you know deeply how it is. I will tell only a small part of that good story. It is a thing that happened to me, one cycle of my life long ago, when I was about seven years old. We had a bad thing happen to our Clan. We were a Clan that did not do any warring at all. We had to defend ourselves from terrible raids by Clans that had their settlements far from our settlement. We were known as a Clan that would not go on the war-path against any other Clan. Of course that made it hard for us, for the bad Clans would pick on us to raid. I was with my father, that morning. "We will have to do something to keep them from coming all the way here," that father said to our old Chief. (He liked me; the wise old Chief and I were good friends. Ordinarily the boy is not with any of the men. Indians were that way, long ago. Women were by themselves, boys were by themselves, girls were by themselves, and men were something special. If the Chief is an old wise ripe Chief, all that means little to him; he is "extra-special".) So it was that my father had let me go along with

1816

him that morning. I was not entirely normal, for I was one who had visions. I would have them as I would be walking along. A drowse would come, and I would be in my vision. Now (be patient with me, reader); when my deep mind says a thing to me, in a tactful way, I take it that I must give good attention to it. I will tell you a thing that may surprise you. Animals too can see those visions. Look up the place in the Bible, that place that tells about the man Balaam; his burro saw the vision before Balaam did.) I was like that burro, me a boy of seven seeing things the wise old Chief did not see. My father, knowing all this, had taken me with him, that very important morning. (My father was Chief of all the Scouts, an important one of the Clan. He himself had gone alone to do that scouting, so as to be very sure those sly base enemies would not know we knew that they were anywhere near our region, our pagus.

I saw it. As they talked, my drowse came on me, and the vision came. It was momentary. But the old Chief had been with his eyes on my face, as my anxious father told how many there were of those fierce bad fighters. "They have many of those grand shining trumpet-things of the bad powerful Yellowlegs people," the Chief-scout said. "Those pushing-all-out Yellowlegs people are managing that bad warring Clan". My good Chief smiled. He was not even bothered by what my father had told. (He was a one who had good use of the deep mind. He, sometimes, himself, had good clear visions. He knew me, who I was, who I was in the Long-life of me – the very old Minstrel who had gone down into the death-sleep some two hands of years before that time. So, of course, our Chief was liking it, when he saw me appear that morning. It was to him a good sign, that I was there that morning. "What is it, Go-Daa?", he asked me (My father had not noticed that I had gone into the doze-state.) I said: "Send me to them!"

The old Chief was in a bad quandry. He would have the blame, of course for my death. He knew that I knew nothing about that kind of scouting. He was back down in the less-deep way of thinking. I saw how all that was with him. I spoke: "If they find a blinded boy, lost and without anything

1817

to eat, and no water, will they do bad to him?"

I was not liking it that they would not let me go. I was in a deep bother what I should do. Three days passed. I was so upset that I felt that I would lose my good way of doing, if I did not be in a quiet place alone for awhile. I was one who was let go out of the settlement when I would do that. I was one who liked the taking of the little band of goats out to new far places, so that they could get good things to eat. That morning I went with the six goats.

It came to me what I would do. I put the six goats with another group of goats, and went. (My father being the Chief-scout, let me know where I would find the big war-party. I ran. All that day I ran fast. (In those times that was a thing that Indians did much of; that was normal, like deer running far if there is the need for that. We did not feel tired even after we had run fast several days. We were like the swift-footed wild dogs were.) I was not liking the having to do that, without the good consent of my Clan. Very bad that would be, if I was not special. I had come to know that I had been the wise old Minstrel, the "yesterday" cycle of my life, so, of course, I went on with that plan.

I will not tell you how things were, in detail. I will tell you only the last, so that you can see how that all came out to a remarkable good end. I did the thing I knew to do (when I had got to a place near to that war-party, where I would hide in some brush). I was not liking to do that, of course. I put much poison-juice in my eyes, so that I would be blinded. I did that thing. Of course the invisible friend was much with me, all the hours of that dangerous time. It would have been very terrible slow-torture among many jeering bad base inhuman men, if they had found me. I did not have any idea how very bad those ones were. Had it not been that one of those enemies found me, and was watching what I (nearly blind) did, I would have been put to that terrible long-drawn-out torture thing. (They used long sharp cactus-needles to do the slow-torture. One a day they would slowly push into some tender place.) If I had been "taken", they would have, first thing, pushed the needles into the eyes of me.

1818

That enemy who had found me picking berries, was good to me. My eyes were not yet entirely blind; I could see a thing, if I held it close to my eyes. How fine that enemy-man was; he knew just what to do. He used the deep mind of him. He said nothing to me. I knew, by the jeopardy-sign, that I had been discovered. (I was in good care, I knew that; the very wise great invisible Friend was right there. Frequently he would be in my heart, as well as in my deep mind, so I would feel the good glow that his being in the heart causes. I was in no feeling of bad fear.) The Indian did a thing. He scratched two marks on a small flat thin pieced of rock, and put that rock into my hand. I held it up to my eyes, and saw the two scratches. Instantly I knew what to do. I called out very loud: "TWO Marks", Indian words that meant that. (That was the name of the bad brutal inhuman Chief of that war-clan.) That thing changed everything. Indians came there. They saw only a small blinded lost starving thirsty Indian boy, one who had been far, to get the kind of berries women use for some of their color-work. I had done too much of that, they thought, so that my eyes had got in a not-good state. I had done the thing that made it seem that I was calling on that Clan for help, me but a lost blind boy. Even the worst one of the Clans was in good respect for the laws of human doing.

I was taken in by the Scouts. They took me to the Chief. He was good to me. He asked me what Clan I was from. I told him. He did not suspect that I had done that thing purposely. He was not nearly as bad as he was thought to be, when you got to know him. What he did going on raids was but old established custom; how could the Chief go against the old established clan customs?

Thought I was but a boy, my being blind and my being a guest of the war-band made them be friendly to me. The Chief got so he like me. I was not in any danger at all.

My eyes got well of that inflammation in a few days' time. I knew it, when it was the time for me to start back home. "Come visit in our settlement," I said to the Chief, as I started off to go to my own pagus.

How could they go on with that bad raid after that? It

1819

was the very thing. Not any other raids ever threatened us after that. I was in good feeling when I got back home, for the thing had been a success. They held a great clan-celebration, in honor of me. They all got to know who I was, from that thing I had done. They gave me the name I had the "yesterday" cycle of my life.

Now, you see how it is. I could have told you that the deep mind is the mind you have grown down the ages of the evolution of life in this planet, and the less-deep mind is only the mind you have formed for yourself by your reasoning and planning this present cycle, a one-cycle mind. How much good would that have done? My story shows how you do, when you go in accordance with what the deep mind of you tells you; you act with the great invisible friend.

In three small things I will wind up this kind of an introduction to my long story. "Be on your guard against putting too much dependence on mere reasoning. Be ALERT, for the great World is ALIVE, not a mere great big place. Be simple in all that you do and think. Nature, the greatest, most noble, of all persons, the one with the most experience in living, is that way, simple. That one it not some "great GOD", a one who likes to be "worshipped". Only a moron would like that. The invisible one is a lowly one, ant to ants, snake to all snakes, fern to all ferns; she likes them all.

A bad thing happened in western North America long ago. That great canyon known as the Grand Canyon of the Colorado river was not made as the geologists believe it was made. I have to go against geologists much, in this own of my stories. (Of course you should not take my say in anything; I am not noted for anything. I am only one of the common people, one of the lowly ones. I can read. I can think. I can do something with the deep mind of me. Take me, or have nothing to do with me, as you feel to do. I am writing a story. In my story I have to go against much that most of the people of this era believe it would be foolishness to deny. I have to be one poor small fish against everybody of the whole human race. I am not now bothered by that. Like my story? If you find that you cannot go along

1820

with me in my story, it will be for you to get out of my company, for I can do nothing for you. If you read all this just to try to pick flaws in it, I can do nothing for you.

I myself was there, when the great flooded salt sea went out. I saw that great strange deep palisaded long canyon being cut out. It took a terrible great catastrophe to do that thing. If the geologic-agent is too weak for the given work, then no matter how many millions of years you allow for that piece of work, that agent could not do it. How could mere mild erosion make a canyon like that mile-deep one is? It seems to be agreed among all the geologists that they will not consent to give credence to any theory that says great "catastrophes" occurred in past eras. They seem to have to explain everything geologic by means of the mild geologic things that are going on now in the earth. They seem to be blind to the facts. I have to speak of this here, for I have to tell something about the great beautiful inland sea that nearly filled Great Basin of North America, before the time of my story. That thing, the going out of the great loved sea - how for centuries many Indian Clans mourned because of that. It was as if a good great intimate personal friend had died, before the time. We all felt that loss deeply.

I was old, at that time. I would not go away when my Clan migrated from the spoiled devastated region. I said to our Chief this: "Let me stay here to do a vigil. You have the good young Minstrel. He will give you the help you need." Our old Chief knew that within a big ring of watching buzzards I would go down to the death-sleep. He knew how deep was the thing that terrible catastrophe had done to me. Dense continuing fogs were there in the region where we had lived in our temporary shelters, that winter. They were there after most of the great sea had gone out. I was in my mind like that, all of a dense continuing "bad dreary dead fog". So, what was there for me to do but sleep the deepest of all sleeps. Only the death-sleep could clear up all that. I had done my work of that cycle of my life.

The last thing before the Clan went away, we had a ceremonial-cleansing of each one of the Clan. Of course that was not a thing we were formal about; each one came

1821

to me when he wished to do that. Even some of the young children, little more than babies, came alone by themselves to me (the very old Minstrel), to be washed all over by him with good clean water. I had done all that. Then, I had the younger Minstrel (the man who would take my place as Minstrel of the Clan), wash me, in preparation for my vigil. The people of the Clan went away.

In three days I heard some person come, in the night. I was in my vigil. I wondered at that. It was the thing my vigil was for, to give me a good sign. I got the good sign: My sad anguished loved Chief had come back. It was so bad with him that he had to leave the Clan to be cared for by another man (one they could make into a Chief in his stead). He too would keep vigil there with me. We did that. We both died soon after that. I was the one to go first, so I do not know how it was with him. We were in vigil, so we did not talk.

I believe he got to a place where he could see some light. Maybe he did not die there. I have a feeling that he did not die at that time. I have only a very faint feeling somewhere deep in my deep mind to show me about that one of the things. His name, that cycle of his life, was "DAAA". He was one of the most remarkable Indians I ever knew. He was so very strong that he could jump very high, much higher than his own head – and, he was that way in the deep mind of him. He was ever reminding me that some one should go see how things were in the far planet from which the wisest ones of the human peoples of this one of the planets had come (very far back, when most of the human ones wore very much hair, and many had long tails). It comes to me that was the way of it. He must have "gone up".

I may have something to say about that strange thing later on in my story, "ascension". Of course there was no magic in that. The things told about in the Bible, the things that are to the people of this era what are called "miracles", were mere nothings, in most of the planets where life had grown up to near its normal growth, normal for that one of the planets. The great World is very much more wonderful

1822

than the people of this planet in these times have any idea of. There were some animals, like mice, that could do like that, ascend from the ground to a place up high, where they had their good safe homes, do it by changing the rate of thrilling of the myriads of very tiny parts of the bodies of them. How great a change in many things that causes. I will not go into that here.

I will tell you that when one of those terrible catastrophes happened, far back in the past, there was a cause for it, a psychologic cause. I have little patience with the mere scientists of these times. It is as though they, the scientists, would tell great Nature how to do. You hear not infrequently how some invention or discovery "improves on nature". Expensive advertisements are shown. The many fine shades of colors of that product are spoken of. The shades are all just so, each one with its distinguishing name, or number. The "plastics" - how wonderful they are. How durable. How tough they are. "nothing known before these times was ever made like that." Many thousands of new chemical substances have been made by the chemists of these times. How they have "improved on nature". I speak of this matter, here in my book. I have to get people up out of their complacency, or what will they get out of a book of this kind? You see how difficult a piece of work I am trying to do - trying to get the blind to see. You must think of this kind of blindness due to not wanting to use the eyes. I wish I could do as I want to do, go right along with my story. But, that could be only if all those who would read my things were like the very ancient Indians were, able to use to the full the deeper purer mind, and go from there, "jump" from the ground off into space, "ascend", go abroad in the great World.

One thing I must have you be very careful about. Be ever very alert to even small accidents. They are good guidances. If you do not know those as warnings, maybe a worse "accident" will happen to you. That is the way things are in great invisible Nature's great body, whole great World. How big the world is - room for all kinds of complacent people for very many cycles of their lives, psy-

1823

chologic-room. Room for them to get so they are sick and tired of their own complacency. A small common tomato, or common potato, should say deep things about great Nature's useful products. The chemists who make the wonderful plastics - who made them?

In the long ago times, the many ones who then made up the great human family were more simple in their ways of doing and thinking. We who now are the ones of the same great family have that ancient simplicity deep within us - for each one of us has lived all down the ages since the earliest times. The fact that you do not recall what you did in former cycles of your life means only that wise Nature has it that way - so that you will not get bored with living in the same planet thousands of years. You are freshened up from time to time. Each time you go down into the death-sleep you forget everything. But, all that is not lost; your experience of the Long-life that you have worked yourself up through is not lost. (How foolish that would be, if Nature let all that go.) You get a good deep rest. When you have rested long enough (years may be required for that), you find some human woman who would be the right one to be your mother. You do what is necessary for getting her to help you up into a next cycle of your life. As you get back those very simple memories, you are in a body suitable for that way of lifing - in the human mother's watery womb. (The human ovum is an amoeba. The mere scientists are blind to that plain fact. They are blind to most of the facts of human embryology.) I must not go into that more here.

In the time that it took for much snow to pile up in many hundreds of miles of mountains, great sad anguished invisible Nature prepared for the bad devastation of many thousands of square miles of western NorthAmerica. Sadness still sits upon all that desert region.

I was standing, years ago, in my deep thought, looking off down into great beautiful Grand Canyon. We, our small family, were in deep feeling while we were there for a short visit. Many complacent people arrive at the rim, and do not even stop talking their shallow talk as they come

1824

upon it. You are disgusted. One man did not disgust me, with what he said. He had said nothing, when he arrived there. He was a thinker. He said, to a friend who was standing with him: "Nature must have had a terrible grudge against somebody, to do a thing like that." It came as a message to me. I needed that, at that time. What a titanic "sign" that is - cut a mile deep in rock. See THAT in your mind, as you go along with me in my story. We are in great need of titanic things - to help get us up out of our smug complacency.

In the few years of preparation for the bad thing that had to be done, much snow fell. The winters were long and cold. The summers were short and cool. Much snow lasted over from the former winter. Glaciers formed in many canyons of the mountains all around Great Basin. That great region has a continuous high rim to it. In the time I am writing of, it was with a rim higher than now, in the place north of the great queer palisaded deep canyon. The southern side of the great ten-miles-wide canyon is about a thousand feet lower than is the northern side. Floodwater more than a thousand feet deep, and many miles wide, did that, cut out that strange great deep canyon, did it in a few months' time.

We were there, that time. We saw that. Our Clan had been warned to migrate up into the mountains. We were camped for the winter above a pass in the southern mountains. We were there when the great sea overflowed.

I should tell you that terrible long-continued rains were for months, before that time. Such rains as the Indians had not ever heard of, kept up day after day for two moons. The sky would be black in the daytime. Great extensive networks of pulsing lightning, and continuous great thunder. Bad big hail killed many people and animals. We had it very bad. We were in terrible deep-vastation all that time. The big hail-stones, high up in the air, reflected the glare of the lightning, so that some of the Indians thought that some of the bad Yellowlegs Gods had got up out of the Underworld, had gone up into the sky, and were casting many burning balls of fire down, to torture the Indians.

1825

In a few weeks, after the break had come, all the sea north of us was a great "canyon-in-the-water". You could feel the rock you stood on give out a grinding feeling. You felt deep strange unearthly fear as you looked off at all that. Vicious bad lightning struck near our camp, terrifying all the not-yet-waked-up ones. We were needing that. Though our Clan had not ever done any of the bad warring, and going far on bad raids, we had to go through some of that. Complacency, how bad it is. We had come, in a subtle kind of a way, to feel "superior" to the people who were still having their settlements within the great zone near the great inland sea, where many Clans were continually having fights. (It had become so bad there that there was no interest in life if some terrible fighting was not going on, or in prospect, so that the many fighters had to do hard stern rigorous practice. It was not enough merely to fight terrible vicious fierce bad tigers, and made almost-insane hounded mastodons; they had to fight the cunningest, most skillful enemies, trained Indian fighters. I will not go more into that. I could write big books full of it.)

The region south of Grand Canyon is much lower than was the great inland salt sea. How titanic the great "spillway" was, when the flooded sea had broken down a wide deep gap in its southern shore. Cubic miles of insane water rushed down every instant. Great long glaciers whizzed down. Mile high, up in the mountains that great sea was. It was that titanic thing made the strange queer deep long wide wound in good old patient Mother-Ground. It was not that Nature "had a grudge" against those bad abnormal human people - it was the only thing that could be done - to get the thinking ones of them to start themselves in on a long much-needed period of deep-vastation. Deep-vastation, the need of that, was what made all that necessary. (In ancient times only something like that flood was needed to get most of the people to take themselves in hand to clean out the badness from the deep mind. Would a catastrophe such as that was do that to people now? Answer that question yourself. Even the very much worse catastrophe, that is occurring now, the worst one that ever came upon the human

1826

peoples, does not get them to do that needed cleaning of the deep mind. You have no hope that a man like the present prime-minister of the British government will get himself started to going through deep-vastation. He will not admit that he is wrong. He is there, he thinks, to do great things for the great British people - so that, next time, they will not be caught unprepared. He is good at using his reasoning-mind.

I was thinking that it was not good to speak out to the people about that man. I was thinking that it was not right to single him out - a man who has done many big fine things for many millions of people. We all like him. We are all grateful to him for what he did. What a great thing it was that he did, during those terrible bad black years. We cannot overpraise all that. I was not liking to do that, cast discredit on him. But, in this book, I must get people to go deep in their thinking. If I did not speak of him, but chose some lesser person to show forth to the people, that would not have been right. Things are as they are, and the thinking-people must see them. I wish too I could retire entirely from view. I like to live far from any city. I do not like cities. I like the wild mountains. I must stay with my people. You do not shirk, especially when the greatest need is for all to be doing some worth while thing. I myself went through terrible periods of deep-vastation. You have to see that you were wrong in some matter; and then do what you can do to make it right, or you cannot get started on that necessary changing of the character of yourself. The man Churchill needs to turn to, and with his mighty will, work on Winston Churchill - till he makes a changed man of him. Maybe he is that man, Nebuchadnezzar. I would not be surprised if he actually is that one, in a cycle of his life, this era. He makes me think of that king. He had much good in him then, thousands of years ago. The good is there, deep in the deep mind of him. Of course he must get rid of all that "king-business". People now in these times know that small communities are the normal units of government. People everywhere are busy forcibly taking back the social-power that had been taken away from them by the custom of "producer-management"

1827

of everything. Powerful centralized governments, with everybody enslaved. I am a believer in the ancient Clan way of living. I see, in the earth-wide "consumer-management" movement, good hope for the restoration of the ancient wholesome satisfying just stable Clan way of life. Centralization of government is always bad. Down the ages that has been tried out. This last great flare-up of that, that the German people and the Japanese people, have compelled the people of the whole human race to be all mixed up in - is but another one of the "grand and glorious" war adventures in which millions of "slaves" are used. We can see that, if we look at things with the long view. The known history of the human race is one long heart-breaking record of "reforms" that failed. This "consumer-management" movement too will fail, if people do not go very much deeper in their thinking than now they are doing. I wish I could do something worthwhile to help many people to do deep thinking for themselves privately. That is why I write this kind of writing.

In the past years I have thought much about the important science of geology. I went, about thirteen years ago, on a long extended journey in our small automobile. My wife and two young children with me, I went. I was (though I did not realize it then) not yet all the way up out of the mild insanity I had been in, that last period of deep-vastation. I was the only one of the party who could drive an automobile. I was in the competent hands of invisible Nature. Great Nature had things to show me, in preparation for this work that I am now doing. I have had to go through some very terrible experiences, in preparation for this work.

I think of a thing that is in the long poem Robert Browning wrote, "The Ring and the Book". I must write some of that out here. Of course he, the deep thinker Browning, should have used strong prose for his important work, not that hard-to-read kind of poetry that he had to get up for his special purpose. Of course I will make prose of that. This is what I wish you to read, and think about. He too could be guided by invisible Nature, a person. "Do you see this square old yellow Book I toss in the air, and catch

1828

again, and twirl about by the crumpled vellum covers? - pure crude fact, secreted from man's life when hearts beat hard, and brains, high-blooded, ticked two centuries since. Examine it yourselves! I found this book, gave a lira for it (eightpence English just). Mark the predestination, when a Hand (always above my shoulder) pushed me once (one day still fierce mid many a day struck calm), across a Square in Florence crammed with booths - buzzing and blaze - (noontide, and market-time), toward Baccio's marble - ay, the basement-ledge o' the pedestal where sits, and menaces, John of the Black Bands with the upright spear, 'twixt palace and church - Riccardi, where they lived, his race, and San Lorenzo, where they lie. This book - precisely on that palace-step which, meant for the lounging knaves o' the Medici, now serves re-venders to display their ware - 'mongst odds and ends of ravage - picture-frames white through the worn gilt, mirror-sconces chipped, bronze angel-heads once knobs attached to chests - handled when ancient dames chose forth brocade, modern chalk drawings - studies from the nude, samples of stone - jet, breccia, porphory, polished and rough, sundry amazing busts in baked earth - (broken, Providence be praised), a wreck of tapestry - proudly-purposed web when reds and blues were indeed red and blue - now offered as a mat to save bare feet (since carpets constitute a cruel cost) treading the chilly scagliola bedward; then, a pile of brown-etched prints, two crazie each, stopped, by a conch a-top, from fluttering forth - sowing the Square with the works of one and the same Master, the imaginative Sienese, great in scenic backgrounds - name and fame none of you know, nor does he fare the worse. From these - Oh, with a Lionard going too cheap - (if it should prove, as promised, that Joconde whereof a copy contents the Louvre) - these I picked this book from." I was not liking to bother you with all that. I had to do some studying myself, years ago, to find out what Browning meant. It is hard to go along with him, so quick and hastening-on is he in his fine good keen unusual mind. We need, do we not, some of that, these times? If you are travelling, and have to do some long hours

1829

of waiting, you need some good thing to help to pass the time more quickly by. Maybe yet again you will go to the busy newsstand (the place where now people go, for things to read). You have no hope; but, an accident might have happened, so that some old classic might be there, in a good reprint. You are nauseated yet again by what you see. The dirty stale monotony of all that shallow stuff. That is producer-management for you. Everywhere you have that, only that. And, you cannot much blame those persons who have to do that tiresome work of tending the stands, for what is there but that kind of stuff? We used to have good wholesome weekly journals. You are sad, when you think of what we have come down to.

Browning was a man who thought to the last deep edge of things, in his own mind privately. And he could do that telling about his things in a fine unusual way. Has any subtle complicated matter forth any more interestingly than that thing about Fra Lippo Lippi - "I am poor brother Lippo, by your leave. . . . "Browning did the things "the Hand" pushed him to; he had some use of his deep mind.

That time, about thirteen years ago, the same great invisible "Hand" pushed me across many hundreds of miles of desert-region. The invisible friend had to do many reminding - me things, so that I would be able to get things back from some important cycles of my life. There was that, and there was the need to see the great extensive flood-plain of that great flood. I went across that. Desert "dry-wash" - what are those millions of square-miles of "dry-wash"? They are in many great extensive regions in many places of the earth. I know, from actual going down into many prospect-holes in some regions, that the material is deep, and that what is below is what you see everywhere at the surface, "unsorted waterworn material". How very much of that there is. What a great unmistakable geologic record that is - of great deep swift floods. I was wishing that I could get clear of the necessity of going into geology, in my story. In a former rendering of this same story, a short rendering, I put most of the geology part in a good appendix. I could not get any book-publisher

1830

even to read my good important book. (They are high and mighty with you. You are as if you were a mere peddler, trying to sell them some of your ware. No matter who you might be, however wise, you get the same kind of treatment from them - unless they can see in you some "easy money").

In the time it takes to say three short sentences, I will see if I cannot "shock" you out of some of your taking for granted that the geologists are always right in what they say. Geologists are silly. Geologists have not yet opened up the eyes of them. Geologists worship "authenticity". I myself am a nothing; I am only one of the many millions of lowly persons. You should not take my say for anything. So, if you believe in the greatness of our hard-working geologists, all of them, "know" is true? I have to do what I have to do. The great grand sad terrible canyon we have been thinking about was not any million of years in the making. I was there when it was cut out. When I quit that cycle of my life, the salt water of the great salt sea had gone so far down in the great sink that I was not sure whether that was water, or only wet mud that I saw, when I looked, sick in my old heart, in that direction. I had to see that terrible devastation. I was not such a one then that I could know how deep the way was that mere scientists go in, this era of human history. We were simple Indians. I had no idea the whole of that great sea would go out. I had thought only the flood-water would go out (all that water the snow and much rain had put into the sea). We, in those times, we Indians, were in the way children are now, simple in our minds. The great sea had always been, as far as we were in any knowing of those kind of things. We thought the bad that many people had done had to be "washed away", by the much flood-water. We thought the great one, Great good Mother and Father of everybody, would wash all the badness even from our good ancient sea - and then, after a while, things would be like they were before. We had no idea that the whole great se would go and not ever return.

There are great geologic records of the flood. The great

1831

canyon itself is but one of the great geologic records. Sand, washed far by the great flood, made a great dam all far across what was then the upper part of the gulf of California: Imperial Valley, below sea level, is part of the upper end of that long gulf. I myself saw the geologic evidence of that. How many hundreds of square miles of sand there are between Calex-ico and Yuma? I was across all that. I thought, in the deep mind of me, all the hard hot dry days of that strange long camping trip. Into my deep mind very many things went, those months. I will say no more about that now.

The Story. You must be not blaming me too much for keeping you waiting. Think of all that bad that had happened in the region of Great Basin, as being in the dim past. Think of me as being a small Indian boy in a next cycle of my life, name not a one that I could be proud of (for I had kept on too long with a bad thing that I did not know enough to get you into the right moods - as we go hop skip and jump, up to a time that I must tell you, in some detail, about.

In the early morning young Indian Wau-Kok, the great-grandson of the old crippled Chief, came to the place of the home he lived in, the home of the Chief. He smelled blood before he got there, so that he was running fast when he saw the dead bodies. Five dead Indians were there. Another one of those bad small raids by the base bad low-minded Chief of the enemy Clan. He saw. In deep grief he knew the two oldest ones of his Clan had been set upon by some of Big-coon's most vivious men. Oldness was, in those times, like a thing apart. Even bad enemies usually spared a very old person, even though that one was a woman. It was like what we think of as "taboo". This bad Chief, Big-coon, was that low in his character that he was not like any of the other bad Chief's of war-clans. He had for years killed off single families of that Clan. That was his "fun". The people of our Clan were known as "carrot-eaters", an Indian word that meant ones who would not eat flesh, but had to do gardening (women's work). and keep goats, and go for berries and nuts and melons and

1832

roots that were good to eat, and store up much things for food. Each family had its private storage-place. Each time the band of raiders got one of those families killed, it was the thing they liked to do to wreck the garden, break down any good nut trees, or fruit trees, and take all the stored-up good things they could find. Burn what they could.

It was the afternoon of that day. A terrible day it was for that Clan. All of the men who knew about that base thing were in a bad rage. A thing like that would not be kept from blazing out into a bad continuing "fire" in the heart. A thing like that could make the big change from being a peace-liking Clan to being a war-clan. In those times, in that whole great good region, many bad bands of war-minded Indians roamed. They did not themselves have good home-places; they were ignorant Indians. If they wanted a place to live in, they took from some other Clan. He had thought that such Indians as the ones who did not eat any meat would do what a "real" Chief ordered them to do. He had gone to old good mild serene big-hearted funny Sai-Kar-Du to tell him he would have to move his Clan from that place. Very old Indians, in those times, usually knew what was to come before the time of that was. So, when the bad evil small-minded conceited Chief, Big-coon, showed up from out his hiding-place near the Chief's garden, the old good Chief knew just how to do with him. Sai-Kar-Du appeared to be very much surprised that time, that a man could be that near, and not be courteous enough to let that be known. "You might at least have said you wanted to hide a while in that place," old Sai-Kar-Du said to him. "I put that good bunch of carrots that you ate there for you. You thought that was an accident. Of course an old one like me can know all that is in the bad heart of a one like you. I will not do what you came to order me to do. Get out of here! I give you three very small bits of time to get out of range of my long arrow. You thought me some kind of a fool. You will find me not anything like you think I am. You may kill many of the not-deep ones of my Clan. You do away with some families. You will be in the worst fix any man of your Clan was ever in, before you close

1833

your small evil eyes in death." The bad Chief, though he was well weaponed, did as mad old Sai-Kar-Du had said. Terror came in his heart, ("Old Chief is a witch man", he thought), and he was away like the wind. Even so, the long arrow got him in one foot. He carried the wound, the bad festering wound, till it was the death of him. By means of that stinking wound, the men of Sai-Kar-Du's Clan could trace his bad goings, even in the dark of night. It got so, if there was danger, that bad smelling chief would go alone, so as to not lead the men of Sai-Kar-Du's Clan on the trail of the flying band of warriors. That was what had happened that time when his men had killed old Sai-Kar-Du; wounded Big-coon had gone one way, and the others of that band had gone a different way.

Much bad had come upon the peace-liking clan. The very old Chief had not been Chief all his adult life, as is usually the case, when things are normal. The Chief, as he gets old, has a younger man as his helper, so that the Clan will have a well-trained man as Chief when the old Chief dies. The long migration had spoiled things with the Clan I was of. Get things clear in your mind. I was the old Minstrel who kept vigil where the break in the southern shore of the great inland sea was, that time. I went down into the death-sleep there. After some years of good deep rest, I came up into the next cycle of the Long-life of me, in a family of the same Clan. At that time they were already settled in a good place near a little pretty lake. Great giant trees were there. Those were giant Redwood trees. The region was what is now known as the coast of northern California. I was not knowing anything about my former experiences, of course. All that was forgotten, as though I had never lived at all before. I had heard stories of how the Clan had to do a long hard migration. They were but stories to me. I was one of a family that had taken, secretly, to flesh-eating, a bad thing to do, even if no wrong had been in that way of doing, for all the families of the Clan must be of the same mind about things, or a bad division of the Clan may grow up. I knew not that to catch rabbits, kill them and eat them, was wrong.

1834

My father did that. Of course to a young boy what his father does is right. It was my "fun" to trap and kill quails. It is only later on that the wrongness of what the young boy's father does is realized by the boy. It is hard for a lone isolated boy to get to know that there is wrongness in what his father is doing. The isolated boy knows nothing about the Clan, except what his father chooses to tell him. It was that way with me the early part of that cycle of my life (the next one after I was the very old wise sad anguished Minstrel, who chose to die where the great flood had ripped a great deep bad wound, long and wide and jagged, in good old Mountain, so that the much water of the pretty blue friendly sea went out forever).

I must tell you that thing being born in that kind of a family did not just happen to happen. I chose to have that be that way -- so that I could know how very bad flesh-eating is. The age-old deep mind of one manages that getting up into the next cycle of life. You need to see the things from the inside of them, if you are to know deeply about them. I will go no more into that now. Of course I could write out in good form all that long story. I did write some of it all out, in preparation for my work.

Wish-Naa-Gaa got here. She was on her way going to the home of the old Chief, when young Wau-Kok ran, in a rage, on the trail of the band that had done that bad thing in the night. She went to that place. She had come the long way there, from her isolated far home, to know why her old greatgrandfather had not returned home, as he was supposed to do. He had promised to be home in time for the good welcome to a small thing that would happen in that lone hidden Indian home. A fine dog, Scout-trained, had come home with a wild "woman" dog. The wild she-dog was in the family-way when she came there. Of course the coming of the babies would be an interesting event, to those two lone Indians, one very old, and the other young. (I should tell you that years before that time a band of Big-Coon's men had come in a bad storm in the night and had killed all they found in that isolated home. Wish-Naa-Gaa, then a young girl, was the only one to escape. In the heavy

1835

rain she went through brush. Dense brush was there. (That was what had hidden that home before that time from the bad enemies. They had watched, at that time, for the going home of one of that family, so those enemies had killed them.) Indian girl Wish-Naa-Gaa was with that in her heart ever afterward, that cycle of her life. The old Chief of the Scouts had been away from the home, that night, so he had not been killed. In the morning, after that bad raid that time years before when he got there, he knew the young girl had made good her escape. He knew where to go to find her. Ever since that time they had lived alone together, as intimate friends. The old Chief-Scout had made a good Scout of her. She had become the wisest Scout the Clan had; for she had good use of the deep mind. She had got away from Big-coon, one time. Easily she made him believe she was very glad he wanted to take her as one of his women. She played that she was in love with him. She easily made him let her pretend that already she was his proud young wife, following along behind him, "so as to make sure no enemies would get on his trail." She was off, without his seeing, up one of those big giant trees, on some great funny strange warts that grew on that old one. She had done that same thing up that same tree many times before, as a child, so she easily knew how to get up away from that very dangerous evil one. That, and many other things, are all in the deep mind of me, as I write this condensed account.)

Purposely, that time, the great invisible friend did not let the wise young woman Scout know what was to come. In the simple pleasure of telling him about the fine three puppies they now had, she had come all the way to try to find old Tsu-Gaa, the Chief of the Scouts, her wise great-grandfather.

Rage came in the heart of Wish-Naa-Gaa when she came upon the dead old-ones there. She ran. Furious against the ones who had done that, she took the wind, as she ran fast to go the far way to her hidden home (for her arrows, and her good throwing-spear). The wind - it told her she was on the stinking trail of Big-coon. She was glad. She

1836

would do the thing she should have done before that time. "I should have done it the first time I saw him," she thought to herself. (She had not killed the bad Chief before that time, because her old greatgrandfather had taught her to not kill except in actual self-defense, or in defense of some other person.) On and on swiftly the Indian Scout ran. Though she was a woman, don't think small of her because of that. She was as strong and tough as any young man of the Clan. With the long arrows that that Clan used, with the small penetrating flint heads, she could easily hit a man-size mark as far away as she could see, if she would take the time to quiet her deep mind in the right way, as the very old Scout, Tsu-Ga had showed her how to do. He, the very old Scout, was one who was the best Indian we ever knew at training young boys the things they had to do, if they were to be good Scouts. "One arrow is all you are allowed," he would say. "See, I have made your mark on the haft of it. Shoot, and get there before your arrow hits the thing." That was how he would start the young eager Indian boy out. Of course the thing to do was to train the boy to be very careful in the way he shot, each time, not waste any shots. And, when you had to jump into a run like the swift wind, each time you shot, you got much good hard practise in jumping quick, and in running very fast. I have to put in these explanations as I go along, so you will get the feeling of how it was to be an Indian, one of the ancient kind of Indians. They had to be ever on the watch against animals much more fierce than any wild animals are now in these times. I could tell many stories of that. I must keep to this story, as well as I can. I have to do things, besides this telling of an interesting Indian story. How bad it would be if I would keep readers from their own sad deep thinking about what is going on now - the worst calamity that ever happened in all time to the human family. I must not be only a mere teller of stories. I must do more than that. I must make good use of my chances, as I go along in my story.

It comes to me that I should tell of a thing that happened to me, not many weeks ago. So down in bad anguish was I

1837

from not being able to get any publisher to put out any of my important needed writings, that I wrote some important needed short pieces of writing, and sent them to one of the weekly journals, "The Nation". (I had that journal in my home during some years, about a decade ago, so I knew it for a good journal). I was not in much hope, but you try out what you can do. I got a personal letter back. It was as I knew it would be; they would not publish any of my work. I was interested in the formal letter the secretary wrote to me. She had her fixed rules to go by, I saw that. She herself like what she had read of those pieces of writing. She thought of those as being in the class "personal essays". They had come out of my own private terrible anguish. She was not wise enough to see that in all that I was showing forth there was the most important matter the human race was ever faced with. People are individual persons. She explained to me that the "Nation" had to concern itself only with "important public matters", not "personal essays". My way of writing did not seem "authentic". I was only some "private" person. I had showed the most important public matter that the whole human race ever had to work its way out of, and the good weekly "Nations" was too blind even to see that what I wrote was more than a mere personal essay. How good it will be when everywhere we have what we know now as "consumer-management", instead of the blind leading of the blind that "producer-management" is. Publishing should be better managed.

In a short time after Wish-Naa-Gaa got back to her hidden home that time, she was ready to go on the long trail after Big-coon, till she had killed him. That was like a vow in her mind. What was her own life, if she had to give it? She would even spend years of her life at that if she had to. Indians are fierce, when they are deeply aroused. We have no idea how fierce the ancient Indians could be, when base bad low things had been done. In that they had the constant help of the invisible fierce great friend, Nature - that very old wise "Indian".

Out on the main trail again, Wish-Naa-Gaa was so full of her rage that the scout in her was all but gone.

1838

Who that has been deep in mad rage is not knowing how that would be? She went fast, head down looking at the ground of the trail, to see if she could see any sort of sign of the passing along there of that bad Chief. She was all in a bad dirty mood in her mind. It did to her what anger always does, blinds the mind. That it was that caused that strange thing to happen to her. She, Scout though she was, did not see that a great tree was down across the trail a little in advance, till she had got to the place. She stopped suddenly, almost startled. She realized at once that she was then in no condition to go on the trail against such a wily bad enemy as Big-coon was. That big sign, the great fallen tree across her trail, had been necessary, to shut her off from going on with that foolish plan, at that time. She should, at least, have slept a short sleep, before starting off on such a dangerous trip. She turned aside and went down the steep familiar faint trail that was there in that place. It was a place she had liked to go to since, as a child, her mother had taken her to gather big ripe berries.

She knew, right away, two things, that the stinking Chief had gone down that trail, and had come back up out of there. She knew that he had gone on from there. She went on down. Almost at once she saw his "message" to her. It was a base low-down fierce thing aimed at her. He would catch her, do that bad thing to her, then slow-torture her in a base low way, till she died the lingering death of slow-torture. With some signs, and a miniature man made of mud, base Big-coon, had said that. One of the signs was the bloody sign of the Chief, Big-coon, a common sign he liked to brag his big brag with, when he had made one of his small night-raids in a storm. He liked to seem to be mysterious, so when he could do that, he did his raiding as if he were the bad spirit of a big storm. I will tell one small thing that will show you how dirty in his mind he was. No dog would think to do anything like that. He dirtied in the good spring the people of that family had used for years, and then bragged about that with a big "coon-track" made in the mud there with one of his hands. He was that kind of a beast. You could hardly call him a man.

1839

When Wish-Naa-Gaa saw what was there - - in that beautiful place at the edge of Water-fall's deep clear pool, she did not get the message she should have got, would have got, if bad rage was not blinding her mind deeply. Run up the small faint steep trail in the tall brush was the thing her mad mind made her do. JUMP, and she was back down in the dense brush, and all very quiet, in a very short time. You would not know where she was hidden. She had to jump backward very quickly to avoid being shot by a bow that was at the full bend near the top of the great crashed-down broken fir-tree that lay dead across the main trail. An Indian had all but let fly at what burst suddenly out on the main trail from the tall brush.

Afternoon had come. These things that I have told you will let you know in your mind how it was that I will now tell you in a short way. How young Wau-Kok came to be there, just at that time, there up on the top of that big fallen fir, and all that was going through his mind, would take up many pages. It was he, not any enemy, who almost shot the long arrow at Wish-Naa-Gaa. He had got there to that place on his way back to the settlement. He had gone another way on the trail of the small band who were going, some of them with bleeding wounds. He had seen, at last, that the band had gone entirely out of their region, for their blood was on the Divide-trail, the one that led up to the pass that would take them beyond the high ridge.

He was on his way back to the Clan by way of the main trail. He got to the place of the great fallen fir. It was a sign. He knew he must stop there. He had come from the other side of it. He was at the same place the woman scout had but just got to. He had but got up on to the great broken fir when noise in the brush brought his bow to the ready. He all but let fly with the arrow at what burst out of the brush. How deep was the feeling of fear in him, when he knew that he had almost shot their woman scout. She was away, back down in the dense brush. He had had but a glimpse of her. He had seen her, the one he had heard stories about. To him now she was a real person.

1840

He was in deep sadness, because of that thing that had happened in the night. He was wishing that he could have been there, to do his part in that hard fighting. He went down the trunk of the great fallen fir. He stood there. Tall brush was there, so that he had to look over the tops of bushes to see down into the pretty place of the pool of the waterfall. He had not seen that place before. It was a good place. Water was important to the ancient Indians. You looked into the clearness of good water to clear your own deep mind. That was one of the things thinkers did, in those times. It was a time of great importance in the clan. The chief was gone, and the chief of all the scouts. No head was there to the clan. The thing to do at a time like that was to have a "called-meeting" of the men of the clan, to try to decide who would be the next chief. (Usually there was an acting-chief already working with the old chief, when the old one was not in the actual doing of the things. Old Sai-Kar-Du had not got any younger man to help him. He and the old chief of the scouts had managed everything. They had got to feeling that some bad things were going on in the clan, so that only old wise men could do the right. It had not been well planned out, what they did. For one thing, they were too much in the way of letting raids be made on the clan. They were not ones to do any preparing for war. It had happened that they had not ever had any of that to do. They would do what they could do to fight parties that came to the settlement, but to send out a strong party of trained fighters to do away entirely with the bad war-clan was, to them, a thing that they must not do.)

All this was in the mind of young Wau-Kok, as he stood there. It was a kind of short vigil he kept. He needed good clearness. It was this way: He himself would be expected to do the deciding about how to get going after Big-Coon: He was next of kin to the old murdered chief. He was like the old chief had been, in not wanting to do any killing. If he would be for that - the matter concerned the whole clan. Of course he wanted to go out after those bad men. Hours that day that was in his mind. It was a complicated matter.

1841

To do that, they would have to have the best war-minded man of the clan as the chief. That one was not a one the best families of the clan liked. He was a flesh-eater, a thing that had to be a secret matter in the clan. He was not wise in his managing men. He was not one to be a wise chief. If he got the clan rest from the raids by war-bands, that would make him a great one, in the eyes of many young men of the clan. Of course what the chief orders, that the men have to do. That would make the great change in the clan from being a settlement-clan, to being one of the war-clans.

None of that would young Wau-Kok go for. Much as he would like to go with a party off after that bad one, Big-coon, he would waive all that - so as not to get the whole clan to being the kind of a clan that leader would make it be. He was the one to speak out about that bad murder that had been done. He would, right at the first of the called-meeting, make them know clearly that he was not in on any of that. He knew that the clan was already divided into two clans, one going in the bad direction, and the other wanting to go in the good, the normal, direction. He was not at all wanting to do big things. He was quiet and wanting not to be in any public things.

Hours the young Indian stood there, not moving. (It was that way with the Indians, long ago. Like a stag, he was alert all that time. No mere idle thinking was going on in his mind. The matter was very complicated. From living in the home of the chief for years, he had come to know well the men of the clan. He knew to a certainty which ones were with his part of the clan, and which with the other. He knew that no one of his part of the clan would want to be a chief. If a strong wise old man had been one of his part of the clan, then, possibly, the division of the clan might have been healed. In his mind he went over all that. He "tried out" in his mind how different plans would be, got the feel of them. He was in deep careful thought.

As he was doing that thinking, he kept his eyes on the things that were there. It was the spring of the year, the

1842

best time to be in that place. It was beautiful there. The waterfall was like a living thing. It was as though it was the life of the beautiful place. Beauty and fresh spring fragrance spoke continuing messages. Blue flowers on the tall bushes gave their charm and special wild spicy fragrance to the air. Cool it was down in that deep place of the great woods. Though there were no giant trees in that place, the younger sequoias that were there were tall. The green roof was high. No deep shade. It was a delightful place.

Out of the bad thing that had happened good things would come; Wau-Kok knew that. He had long wished that the clan would separate into two clans. (If the old chief had not been a cripple, and the old chief of the scouts near to blindness, the thing would have been done before now.) "Now is the time for that, the young Indian thought. He was in deep thought for a while, his eyes on the deep clear poll. He was thinking that all that clearness would come to the minds of his part of the clan, if the separation would be made. He was for doing that. He knew how hard that would be; for his part of the clan, being in the minority, would have to give up their homes and the good place to live in, and migrate. He was not in any liking of that. He was thinking they would not have it easy. The clan would be small. Too many of them were young persons. No good old man was there to be the chief. Migrating puts bad strains on everybody. The wisest chief cannot do very well when the clan is on the long trail. Each one has to be burdened with a big pack. Even the children would have packs. No good places to camp could be hoped for, for they would have to lead a hidden kind of life: You do not do fighting when you are migrating - children, women, goats and all that. It was not any good feeling that was in the mind of Wau-Kok, as he thought of what they would have to do. They would get away from the bad things that the war-clan liked to do to them, that was one good thing. He, Big coon, would do much worse, now that he had been all but defeated by the two old men of the clan. (They had not been caught unprepared. They must have done quick work in the dark, to have killed

1843

three of Big-coon's chosen men. He, the bad chief himself, had had to go with a bad wound from the fight at the first. The two old men were fighting fiercely to the very end. The men who did get away were bleeding with wounds.

Wau-Kok remained in his vigil. Though it would be only a short one, he needed deep help in all that that he would have to do. He was wishing his short vigil would give him that help. He had thought that he would have to do alone what he had planned to do, that speaking out at the "called meeting" of the men of the clan.

He was, you might say, almost taken by surprise by the thing that suddenly happened. Though he was a scout, the thing get done before he fully realized that any other person was there. He saw the back of the head of the woman scout as she stood up down near the pool. He had been in vigil, and this had come. This meaning came to him: "Not only the old chief had been killed, but the great grandfather of the best scout the clan had. Though she was not a man, surely, in this case, she should be one of the ones to speak out when the meeting was. The two of them, next of kin to the ones who had been killed by the bad band, were the ones to speak out first." He needed to tell the woman scout about what had happened, and urge her to go to that meeting. It would need some talking to get her to see that. He was not liking it that he had been there all that time, she being in hiding somewhere. (He had supposed that she had gone away.)

He looked at her. He had heard the stories that were told about what she had done. (He knew about the good home she had kept for the old great grandfather - how she liked to do woman-work, weaving pretty colored things, and doing the necessary things in the home, and in their garden. She was "woman"; and yet she was fierce "man" when it was the time for that. She had killed a big bear. No easy thing for even several strong men. She made good use of her deep mind. That was how it had come about that she was the best one at scouting of all the scouts of the clan. That bear - it was simple what she had done. When she knew she had to kill the great beast, she ran right up to him, as

1844

though to do a great rush at him. The thing so surprised the bear that he was in fear. He was not used to that. Usually things got quickly out of his reach. That time, he did not do anything with his great powerful arms. It was as though he wanted them to protect himself from what might come. He rose quickly up on his hind legs, to meet what was to come. The great mouth was wide open. Wish-Naa-Gaa's spear was run into his mouth and she was away with a great quick jump. That was all there was to it. Not the least bit of fear had clouded her mind. She was that way, without any fear.)

It was not good to stay on here. But, Wau-Kok was in vigil. You wait for the wise old invisible friend to release you from vigil. He knew that they both were in the hands of the old one. She did not know he was there, back up on the base of the great fir that had been blown down. He was all but hidden by the tops of the blue flowering bushes. He was not to take any responsibility on himself for that. Though it might seem that he was looking into the privacy of that young woman's life - he was in vigil. He had not wished to do that. He had not had any idea that she was still there. And, there was that needing to talk with her about going to the called-meeting, with the men of the clan.

A thing happened. It was a delighting thing. It was, Wau-Kok knew, a sign given to that fine wise young woman. He was in fine good fortune, he thought, that he had been permitted to be there. It came to him that the great invisible Father was there. It came to him, that Wish-Naa-Gaa too was in vigil. It was a very unusual thing. The person goes where he can be away from any other person, when he is to do vigil. He had been in vigil, and she, not knowing that he was anywhere near, also went into vigil. He saw what Pool saw. He wanted to be with his eyes away from that. It was too private, he felt, for any man's eyes. It was an intimate woman-thing. He was seeing how the great understanding invisible Father spoke a fitting message into the heart of a pure young woman. He was not let turn from that.

It was this way: Pretty Falls was the one that great

1845

Father used. Those pretty falls were, to Wish-Naa-Gaa, like a human friend. She had played there many times as a child, before her mother had been taken from her. It was her favorite play-place, when she was a young girl. She had gone there not a few times to get berries with her mother. All that was in her mind. She had often felt as if her mother would look up to her, from very deep down in the clear pool. You who now read this should know that in ancient times persons were much more simple and direct in their ways than now any people are. Like children they were. It would be the thing to play that her mother was with her when in after years she would go to that one of the places she liked. She had her special places in that region that she knew well, and liked. (The having to kill that bear, that time, had spoiled for her one of her places, a place where she had done much work, to make a pretty thing in honor of great Sun).

How much there is to tell. I could write a good book full of the things the Girl, Wish-Naa-Gaa, did, all alone, in the great wild woods. How fair she was to all her animal-friends. She had had big "WUMPAA", a mother-bear for her friend. She would hunt her out, to go with her. They both liked berries. WUMPAA knew where to go to get the best ripe berries. There is a good story to that - how she came to be accepted by the wild mother-bear. "Kreak" was one of the small friends, a particular tame cricket. Lizard friends, and spider friends, and beetle friends and fish friends, all those helped the lone Indian girl to grow, in good ways - as she was in the wise care of the great invisible Father and Mother.

Pool did a singular thing, or was it Pool? I am thinking that it was the mouth of the pretty falls. Think of Falls as being with her feet up over the top of the ragged hoary dark-colored small cliff down which the water did not quite fall, but ran very fast. All a glint was the thin sheet of pure clear cool water. That was the body, you might say, of Falls. She was the life of that place. She had come there, very long before that time. See what she had done there. She had even done things to the hard rock of the small

1846

precipice, if you could call so small a jumping-off place a precipice. Ferns, lacy ones, were all about the clear stream as it came over the top of the old rock. How pretty the water had made the whole place. Of course what made it be very fine (almost the best of all the things) was the mirroringpool the waterfall had dug out. Now that I have got you to see something of how it was, I can go on. Falls was there, hanging down so that she could just kiss the surface of the big pool. She was ready for the doing of that very special thing. Before the coming of the discouraged young Indian woman, Falls had been talked to by the great one, the great invisible Father. She, Falls, wanted to do something to help the Indian woman to get up out of her despair (So bad was it that she was thinking to kill herself.) Pool was to help with that. It was a thing delightful. It was a fairy kind of thing. It was as though the pretty Falls kissed the face of Pool - and something happened. A few times the same thing happened: "Boooooooooooo-uble."

Wish-Naa-Gaa had not ever seen any pool do a thing like that before: Glittering beads shot out from impact of falls on pool. Radiating strings of pretty beads went out from the central part of the small falls, slide, slithered out over the smooth surface of the pool, many beads in rapid succession - a delighting thing. How could that not be a sign? Wish-Naa-Gaa had but gone into vigil there - and that had happened. It was repeated. Three times the same thing happened. A deep peace came into the heart of the despairing young woman. Again, there at that place, she had come upon peace. Yet again it was as if her mother was down in that pool. It was as though she felt her presence there. In deep thought she looked into the clear water. All of her sad past she saw in a kind of a way. Her child-years were there. It came to her: "Pool gives back things." Each glint and glow the water mirror gave back up to her- the great long trunks of the few trees quivering, because of the small waves of the pool. It came, just then, as a surprise thing - a new sign! "Bright-sky" looked up at her, from deep in the Pool. It was like a good omen. From

1847

black despair, she had been got quickly up into good hope. It was to see what was to come, in the bright future the good invisible Father was showing to her. She was at a time when she needed to know what was to come. (She had thought to go down into that pool, do that terrible thing - so as to get to be with her mother again. Her one human friend was gone. It was as bad as that, to her. She knew no other person in the clan. Her clan! She had had but one person, and he an old man - only that. And he was gone. How could she go get herself into the clan? In a bad bitter feeling not long before that time, in her hiding-place in the dense brush, she had even thought of the possibility of killing herself there with her spear.)

Bright-Sky (that person) came to help. She looked down from above into the mirror. Old Sun did that. (How he liked Wish-Naa-Gaa! He and she had had many serious times together). In two other quick happenings the great truth dawned on the young Indian woman. Deep peace was within her. Two small pretty butterflies were suddenly there, near a pretty flower the fragrance of which Wish-Naa-Gaa liked. (She had looked there to that place, to see yet again that pretty blossom. It was a lone one. It showed how it loved the pretty misty falls by leaning toward it, and pointing with its pretty flowering fragrant tip up to it.

A quick glance got the Indian young woman to be just in time to see the color - FAIRIES, was what first came into her mind. They had seemed to come right out of the air. One sip at flowering tip, and whirling together, up they went fast on their way. She had had to be quick with her look, to see in what direction they went. Up the glinting falls she saw the flash of color go. Her eyes fixed on the two happy twirling butterflies, knowing well that they would tell her of things soon to come in her own life. A strange glowing was in the woman-heart of her. She knew what that meant. How much she wanted to have a home of her own, with a good man, and children. It was to be! She was sure of that. (Who it was she would mate with she had no idea at all. She had had no young man to talk with ever. She had hardly seen any of the young men of the clan. She had

1848

gone far, one time, to try to find some other clan. That had been frustrated.)

It was far above that place that the window in the high forest canopy was. No low branches were anywhere in all the reach up through which the two pretty fluttering butterflies went. She, the young Indian woman, had a clear view all the way up to the high window. They went out at that window. It was a sign. It was sure prophecy. She was in vigil, so she was sure about that. The great Father, knowing well her deep need, was definite and clear to her.

She looked down. Deep into the clear water she looked. It was as though her mother spoke the message up to her: "You will marry, and go far from here." A good glow was in the woman-heart of her.

She had let fall her bow. She stooped, took it up, and went up the steep trail. She was met, when she went out of the brush onto the main trail, by Wau-Kok. It was only then that it came to him that he was the one. (He had seen what the message was that had been given to the young woman. He had had no thought that he was the one.) He looked into her face. She looked into his face. They KNEW.

One small explanation is needed. It was near night. There would not be any place in the settlement ready for the coming to it of two strangers. Wau-Kok thought that his aunt might take them in, till they would be with a home of their own. He was, of course, shy in the presence of this young woman; (he had had nothing to do with woman since his own mother had been killed). He was in no knowing what to do. She was knowing how it was with him. She was the one to make the decision. She told him to go home to the settlement. She would come, the next day, with some of her things, to see if the aunt would have room for her in her home. It was that way. The aunt felt honored by that wise handling of the matter.

Far from there they are, that part of that clan, in this that will now be what my story will tell something about. I have to go it hop skip and jump in parts of this book. If I should write out all that I have, in years past, written out about the ancient-Indians, it would be many books.

1849

It may be better just to give some of the things: The people of these times do not know anything at all about that time. That being so, my books would not be read. I want to do a short book, one that ordinary people might like to read, and like to think about. My way is to do things with stories. People like stories. I am not good at making up stories. I get all my stories from out former cycles of the long-life of me. I feel sure made up stories are not literature. I may be wrong about that. Let that pass. It will be a thing no one can be sure about till several centuries have passed. I thing that what lives on is literature. The important things continue on. It is that way in the deep minds of everybody. My idea about literature is taken from what I know of the deep mind. The "you" you are, the PSYCHE, is a wise knowing "librarian". Do you think that one would clutter up the "library" the deep mind is with things that had been merely imagined, had not actually been lived? Actual experience is the thing, in the long-life. Wise invisible Nature knows best how to do. But very complicated are many human things that even Nature herself cannot know beforehand how all will come out. Human experience is a very rich field to work in. It does not ever grow old. It is what it was at the time. Persons do not change in the deep things of life.

In a few years, the part of a clan was but a wandering band of discouraged Indians. One thing after another had happened to keep them from settling down in a settlement. No place that they could be safe in was good. We can know how it is, if we think of one of the war-stricken countries; no place was safe from bands of raiders. It was like that at that time. The devastation that the great flood had caused sent all the Indians who had lived anywhere in that whole great region west, or east. Of course as good a region as clans would want to live. Thousands of Indians migrated there - "refugees" from the great flood. A few war-clans could spoil everything for all the clans of Indians. War-bands ranged far and wide, raiding their way where they found any settlements to attack.

That was one thing. Another thing was that no good

1850

feeling about who should be the chief had come to the families of the clan. They were a clan without any chief. The big older man wanted to be the chief. He was not the one for it. He and his wife were "ambitious". It was, of course, not good. Most of the families wanted young Wau-Kok to be the chief. (Though he was young, he was one who had good use of the deep mind of him. And he would have the help of the woman scout, Wish-Naa-Gaa.) The one ambitious family was always making trouble in the clan those bad hard years. At the very time in the lives of those ones when noble-minded harmony was much needed - there was none. What could you do against that? Such persons are blind in the deep mind. Of course any person who would want to push himself forward to be the chief of a clan would be one most unfit for that important work; only a person who had good use of the deep mind could do that work well. Only the invisible friend should choose the one for chief. (He, the big man, should have remained with the other part of the clan. He knew that he had no chance to be chief of that larger part of the clan, so he joined with the migrating smaller part of the clan. He had thought that they would be glad to have him be the chief.) He was that way, blind in the deep mind. He was one who would reason things out. He would not see why the other families went against his plans. Several years they were on the go.

Wise Soo-Maa-Hillo, the oldest woman of the clan (the woman who did no talking at all), was like an old chief in the clan. She it was who decided what to do, at the most difficult times. The families all knew that she would get them out of the bad state they were in. They trusted to her. You would go be with her awhile - and you would know how she thought, what she wanted you to know. We all had good use of the deep mind, so that mere words were not needed. (Of course she was one who lived apart; she was not one who was, at that time, active in clan matters.)

I will tell you what I heard, for I was in a place near where Soo-Maa-Hillo came to, that very early morning. I was posted there to keep watch, back a small way in some

1851

brush. She did not know anyone was near. I was almost in a doze, when I heard her not far away. I saw her, and knew her, in the dim light, for our best-liked one of all the clan. (She was at that time, the one the clan looked to for wise counsel, for young Wau-Kok, our chief, had been away a long time. We were thinking he had died.) She was in some agitation, I could see that. She kept putting her head far up in the air. It was a singular thing. I had not ever before seen her do a thing like that.

We had been all deep in anguish. (I will have to tell you some thing of that, before I go on with this thing.) Our young chief, Wau-Kok, had been struck by the big older man who had felt that he should have been chosen as the chief of our part of the clan (when the clan had split into two smaller clans). He was a good man. We all liked him. But he had a big idea of himself. He would not cooperate with the one we wanted to be the chief. He made trouble all the time. We had had much trouble ever since we had set out on the migration from the good settlement. We had thought that we would not have to go very far away, to find a good place where we could make our own settlement. We were not able to get any place that suited all the families. The big man saw to it that some of the families wished to find a better place. It got so that the young chief, Wau-Kok, was despondent all the time. Worry, if it continues a long time, makes the person unable to have good use of his deep mind. We, in those times, depended on the signs we got from the invisible friend (great wise understanding Nature), for all the important moves of the clan. We were, in a kind of a way, like what you think of when you think of the "Children of Israel" as they went their way in the long journey forth from their bondage in Egypt; we too were looking for "a promised land".

Of course "the pillar of cloud by day, and the pillar of fire by night", was not any outward thing; it was no magic thing; it was a thing in the deep mind of the able Leader of that great sad unsatisfactory migration. I wish more thinking-persons would look down into the old stories of the Bible - with no religion at all in their minds.

It may seem out of place in this story, but it is the thing

1852

in this book to try to get persons to think into things for themselves. I have referred to one of the old stories of the Bible. Migration is much in the minds of people now. How could I be doing good work in this book if I did not go into matters that are important to many millions of people at this time? It may be that some persons will be on a migration while they are reading this book. Moses was one who led many thousands of people on a long-drawn-out migration. Many millions of people know the story. I want to make use of that old story. It is one that should show millions of people how not to do. We have seen how the German people and the Japanese people tried to do that very thing - go take the good land that was the land of another people: The tribes that inhabited what the Israelites thought of as "their promised land" had that as their loved home-land. How would any supernatural great one do a thing like that? The idea that some great "GOD" gives a people the right to go take the homes away from the people who made the homes is, of course wrong. Moses made a bad mistake. It is that mistake that I want to point out to you. Wars of conquest are "justified" in the minds of millions of people, because of what Moses led the Israelites through the wilderness to do. The millions of religious people who take the Bible to be some kind of a "God's great book", a thing to be almost worshipped, have done great harm to the whole human race. War is a very terrible thing. We need to see clearly that there never was any real justification for any war of conquest. (Of course I would not have you think that I am against war. If you are set upon by some other people, you should make war against them.) I am speaking about war in general. The thing should never have been. It must be understood clearly, if we are to get anywhere toward getting rid of it. If you listen to such men as Roosevelt, or Churchill, or Stalin, you will be borne down by the great force of the arguments.

Moses was brought up in the home of a queen. Do not forget that. Early in his life he was taken away from the home he was born in. He had his own mother to be the one to care for him; but no feeling of being a lowly person could

1853

he have. He was from the first "a favored one". His own people did not like the way he did, when he was a young man. His idea was that he would rescue his people from slavery. It was good. He did well to want to do that. He had the big idea that he was the one to do that. He was not good at it. His first move was a boy thing. He had made no great plan. He was not at all one who would understand his own people; he had not lived with them. He had heard about them. What his mother told was, to him, stories about his people. He was full of stories. He must have known the old stories of all the great ones of the Israelites. He was like a prince in a royal family. The delivering of his people from slavery was a dream of a prince. You must do thinking yourself, if you are to get down to the actual facts. For so long have people everywhere thought in a certain way, that to think any other way seems to be a wrong thing. I want to do justice to Moses, not unjustness. It is too serious a matter to let lie as it has been for thousands of years. There is always this for millions of good people to base back upon: "Moses believed in a war of conquest. God told Moses to make war on many tribes of people." How terrible some of those things were. Tribes were exterminated. Trouble still sits over all that land, because of what Moses did, thousands of years ago. Many millions of good people are now thinking that wars will always be. I need to do more than merely say that wars of conquest are never justified. It would be too bad to take this matter up, and not be thorough in my going down into it.

There are three human rights. Private-privacy is the first of the three. Each individual person has a right to himself. That does away with all kinds of slavery. Having "a job" makes you a slave. "Jobs" require slaves. Providing "sixty million jobs for people" does the same as making sixty million slaves would do. Clans, small clans of friends, federated together, could do all the work of earth-wide industry. Free persons could do all that. The unit of government must be the small clan. "Consumer-management" of all public affairs could take over things right now, and lead on toward what should have been, all

1854

down the ages. Powerful centralized governments should never have been. Families in small clans was what used to be, many thousands of years ago. What badly spoiled that way of living was the easy thing, flesh-eating.

The second fundamental human right is the right of each man and woman to marry. No normal life can be without that. The man has to be mated with a woman to be "complete". That is so as to his body. It is much more needed as to his mind. He needs to be in a family of his own. A wife and children are needed, to get the man to be what he should be. He has to have the good influence of his wife. Women have one kind of mind. Men have another kind of mind. For many thousands of years men have been away from that finer, gentler, more intimate kind of living that the care of the home and of children requires.

The third fundamental human right is the right to have your family be one of a group of families the interests of which are about the same - with no possibility of other different kinds of families moving into the group, without the permission of the whole group of families. No mere property-interests should be let gain control. It should be a real clan. Control over all things there should be in the persons themselves of the clan. All the social-power should be in that small normal unit of government. The clan should be federated with other such clans.

This that I have written out, if it was in force all over the earth, would prevent all wars. Wars result because of breaches of those three fundamental laws of Nature. I need to go into the matter of wars, some. I will do this by showing you something more about the man Moses. He caused some bad wars. Many millions of people seem to think that because Moses did that, long ago, wars of conquest are right. The Germans, and the Japanese, could "justify" what they have done, by pointing people to what Moses did. It is the thing, therefore, for me to go into the matter, a little.

Moses was a prince in the Egyptian court. He had been taken from among his own people when he was yet a baby. He was not really one of the Israelites. It is true his own

1855

mother was his nurse. It was that fact that got him to think to try to be the great deliverer of the Israelite people. They had been slaves to the Egyptians for many years. Moses wanted to do big things. He knew nothing about the lives slaves had to live: Going among them as one from a higher rank in life cannot give you the true feeling; you have to yourself live that kind of a life for years with no hope of ever getting out of it, to know how it is. He was to try to help them "from above". What he should have done, of course, was to go to be a slave himself, and work down there at that difficult years-long preparing all the people for the new life they would have to take to, after the great uprising had been done. He was not much more than a boy in that. He was to be the great LEADER, he thought. They were to do as he ordered. He was that kind of a man. To show you that I am right in this, I will write out a thing that is in the Bible. It is a thing that shows what Moses was actually like. It is "inside information" about him. He had got "the great commission from the great God of the Israelites". He believed that he was "the chosen" one to go do a great deliverance of his people. He was on the way to Egypt. They were at an inn. He would not take his two young sons back to the people to see, they not being circumcised. He ordered his foreign wife to circumcise them. I will write that out: "And it came to pass by the way in the inn that the Lord sought to kill him. Then Zipporah took a sharp stone and cut off the foreskin of her son, and cast it at his feet, and said: 'Surely a bloody husband thou art to me'." Human rights were violated there. He, Moses, was that kind of a man. Should we do wars just because he believed some GOD told him to go into them? If we should go to Hitler, probably he would show you that he had that idea. The Emperor of Japan probably believed that he was one specially commissioned by his GOD. Fundamental human rights are what we all need to go by. Powerful centralized governments are against the three fundamental human rights. That is a fact. The unit of government has to be a small one, in order that no breach of any one of those three fundamental laws shall become a customary practise. What good, then,

1856

can all the grand plans of the big governments of the earth do? What we need, we many millions of common ordinary people of the whole human race, is to get so we see clearly that all big centralized governments must be, eventually, done away with.

In the story, I was in my place in the brush, that early morning. A bad thing had happened. We were all badly depressed by it. I had had to kill one of the men. How bad a thing of that kind is in a group of families that has been on a long hard migration for more than two years. He, the big man, had gone into a rage. He had thought that he should not have to do work, like the other men of the small clan. He was thinking of himself as being the privileged chief of the clan. He was not our chief. He had put himself into that place. Young Wau-Kok was the chief. Wau-Kok would be reluctant to give orders to any person. He was too mild. He was no good as a chief.

What had started the trouble, that time, was Wau-Kok's asking the big man what he wanted to do, stay with the women and children to protect them, or go scout for a good place for the winter-quarters of the clan. That was nothing to get mad about. Of course it was the not being considered the one to send the men to their work; he was not being considered by the clan to be their chief. He must have just let himself go, that time. He cursed. He blamed young Wau-Kok for all the bad things that had happened to the clan since they had set off on that long migration. So crazy-mad did he get, that he pulled off a piece of root, and went for Wau-Kok with it. I killed him.

His wife bit the chief, lying there, in black despair. Wau-Kok had seen what I did. He had not wanted that to happen. He was thinking that the bad wounds the big man had already made on his shoulders with a big club, and the tearing off of a part of his nose by one of the mad swings of that piece of a root, would get that angry man to get control of himself. He was now being set upon by the angry ambitious hating-him woman. Of course men pulled the woman away. Soo-Maa-Hillo killed her, with a swift sure blow with her mad fist she knocked her to the ground, and

1857

killed her with a spear. We thought that, at last, all that bad trouble was at an end. Not so. Wau-Kok, the young chief, felt that all that was due to some deep fault in him. He went right away, got up and went off on the desert. He was bleeding from his wounds. He was not back, next morning. We thought, of course, that he had gone to keep vigil, for a few days. You know how that would be. In those times that was the expected thing. We who were the leaders of the clan not infrequently did that. Of course, at a time like that, the vigil might be a long one. Of course you do not go look for the person who is doing that.

We got troubled, when a whole moon had passed, and he had not come. His anguished wife was great with child. How bad it was, that all this should have happened at that time. This, all this, will put you in the knowing something of what was in the wise old woman's deep mind, as she came near, that very early morning. She had done a thing I did not know the meaning of; she had put one hand high up above her head. She was, I saw, in strange great joy. She talked. (How queer that seemed to me. "Soo-Maa-Hillo is speaking out through the mouth of her!") I was thinking that I would let her know I was there. But, time was not given for the doing of that. She poured forth words. It was as though she had become insane, and had to pour out some words. She had held back from that all the years. How good it was to hear her. Some of the words I will write out here: "GO-da, nee, NAAA bi do GA in tooooooooooooooooooooo, WAU-kok, Wish-NAAA-Ga".

I could go on with that, give more of that. (You should be told that now, this cycle of my life, I knew very little of what the ancient words mean. Of course all that is of the less-deep mind. You have to learn all over again the language you spoke when you were but a hand of years back in the long-life of you - such things as that you do not carry over from one cycle of life to the next one.) Great deep joy was in her. What was it?

When she had passed on from there, so that she would not see me, I got up from my place, and went. It was very early in the morning. (I had been surprised that anyone was out that early from any of the separated camps of our encampment.) I went to the abandoned camp of Wish-Naa-Gaa. When I got there they both were there. Great joy was in me. I do not remember any time when greater joy and peace came to me – because of any clan-thing. I went there. It was in awe that I went.

She, Wish-Naa-Gaa, too had gone away. We were in great anguish because of that, for she was not far from the time of the birth of her child. I had sent out many small parties, to try to find the place of our chief. It had gone on too long, his vigil. You do not eat, if it is a serious vigil you are in. I was fearing that he had got so weak that he had not been able to do what was needed to get him food, so that he was starving. He had taken no water. It was a bad thing, the whole thing. I had the responsibility of the chief's work on me, while he was away. I was the one they all looked to.

I had got so bothered by everything that I had planned to move camp to a place where we would be able to get along, during the winter. (It was late in the fall; flurries of snow had warned us that we must be getting things right for more snow.) I was very busy, those days. In continuing anguish, I had to try to keep my own troubled feeling out of sight. I had the feeling that everything would, somehow, come out all right. But, things dragged on and on and on. I was very much in need of a good long rest myself. My wish was that we, my wife and I, could go off for a private time by ourselves, where we could talk things over whole days at a time. (I was one who knew enough to take and use the good things the best women of the clan had to give. It was not a usual thing for the Indian men to talk with any woman, when it was in the presence of some ones from any other family. I would have got good advice, if I could have had frequent talks with my own wise wife. We had little chance, there in that open encampment, for any privacy. We had given the chief the only private place there was there, for his camp.)

I had done all the things I knew to do to try to find the chief. Some of the men were so bad in their minds that they

1859

seemed to believe that old Soo-Maa-Hillo was some kind of a bad witch: (She was the only one of the clan who did not seem to feel hopeless about the bad things that had happened to the clan. And, she had a way of doing strange things, there in her separated camp. She had lived alone for many years. Her husband had gone away many years before the clan had split into two clans.) We had done what we could do about the chief. We had to take care of the clan. Deep snow would make it bad for us, there in that place. I was compelled to move camp before we knew about Wau-Kok. Some of the men believed he had died.

I was anxious to get things settled, so that I could go myself and make a very careful search for my loved intimate friend. (He was like a brother to me, a younger brother. I was wishing it had been me the big man had set upon, instead of the patient peace-liking young quiet-minded chief. I was fiery. The big man would not have been able to go far against me.) I had done the last thing, had made some few signs on one of the big rocks near the spring, so that Wau-Kok, if he came there, would know where to go to find us. It was the best I could do, till I could go out myself and make a long search for his place of keeping vigil. Who would have thought would happen the thing that did happen? Of course had I had the chance to talk things over with my wife - she would have explained things to Wish-Naa-Gaa, and would have stayed on there at that place with Wish-Naa-Gaa. Why did I not think of that myself? My not thinking how that would be on Wish-Naa-Gaa, was a very bad thing. You know how that would be. Though she knew that was the wise thing to do, when she saw the signs I had scratched on the big bare surface of that rock, it came over her that the whole clan had given him up for dead. She broke down then. Before that time, she had kept up, feeling that he would get back to her before the baby came.

She had had a hard time, the two bad years of the long going in the desert. (Wish-Naa-Gaa was not like any of the rest of us; she was one who was not used to having people about her; her life had been spent in lone goings in the deep

1860

woods. What she had to put up with there on the desert those years was about as far away from that girl-life she had lived as it was possible to get. Of course she did not like any open region. She longed all the time for the cool beautiful woods.) She had bravely put all that behind her, of course, when she became the woman of a family of the clan. You would not ever hear from her any tones that would tend to discourage people. She had a way of making fun of things, so that often the women would laugh, laugh even when the going was very hard, and things seemed to be almost impossible for the whole clan. "No good being like a COOO, Daa-Gaa-Taa," she said, one time when the wife of the biggest man of the Clan was trying to find some better way to do the small knot the women liked to do, as the last one of a piece of knitted-work. The women all laughed, though before that time no one was even thinking the clan would escape from the flood that had come to shut us in on a small island in a flooded draw. (A sudden unexpected cloud-burst had quickly brought a flood to our camp.) The Indian word "COOO" could be taken in either one of two ways; you could take your choice. It was serious, if you wished it to be, or you could take it the other way. I was not far away. I had to laugh out, so that those women knew that I had heard. The serious way was this: "No good being a dead-one in a pretty knitted death-bag". The other to take it that it was very funny: "No good being a little-bubble". The thing came just right. Nothing could have been funnier. The woman, Daa-Gaa-Taa, was the big woman of our clan. She had had to be in the flood, floating along in it, to get back to camp from far up the draw the quick flood had rushed down. She was not the one to let a thing like that keep her from going on with her knitting, when she had got dried at the big fire the women made for that purpose. She too had a good streak of fun in her.

We had all been deep down in sadness. Wish-Naa-Gaa had gone away! She was not in her camp when I went there, next morning after I had made those signs on the rock by the spring. It came over me then what I had done. I was blaming myself, of course. We went out to find her.

1861

We had no thought but that we could easily do that. How strange it was; we could not find any tracks in the snow to show where she had gone. I was so bad in my mind that I was almost sick. (I might have known she would stay on there, in the dense brush of the thicket that was near her hidden camp.)

I was warned by Wish-Naa-Gaa, after the thing was past, not to tell any one what she had done. She had had no thought that the clan would stay on there. She would not go from that place; her Man might come there all weak, and would be in great need of her help; that was what she had thought. She had it very hard, that time, hidden in the brush. She was knowing that what she had done was making the clan stay on there, in deep mourning for her, as well as for the chief.

Now, I will go back to where I had to go from, to make all these explanations. I had gone, quick, to the camp. I was weak in my knees when I saw that both of them were actually there. I saw that the chief was not "all there". He still had the wild look to him that insane persons have. So, warned by that, I was not at all showing any surprise.

"Got back at last, did you, Wau-Kok," I said to him. He was so thin that I was frightened. Wish-Naa-Gaa, great joy in her heart, was trying to get him to swallow some thin gruel, such as only small babies have to eat. He was wild in the eyes. I took things into my own hands. Almost he was for going away. I saw that he had all but passed out, from being far down in terrible deep vastation. I had not once thought of that possibility, or I would not have been as much bothered as I had been. Now, it came to me: I knew why it was old Soo-Maa-Hillo had not been much troubled by what was happening: She had known all along that the long hard journey the clan had had to go on, two hard years, was a kind of deep-vastation for us all. Of course the chief, and the wife of the chief, have to go deeper down than does any other person of the clan - except the minstrel of the clan. I myself had not been feeling that it was a good thing, all that had happened to the clan. By that time I had come to believe that we were in the

1862

wrong, in some way, some hidden way, or things would not have been so bad for us. You get sick of going on the desert. We had not been too fond of the desert at the first, of course, for we were woods-Indians. We had come to hate all that by that time. We had not yet known that the great deep wide long canyon was not very far to the north of our place. My wife was the first one to find that terrible wonderful remarkable deep thing.

One other thing I must say here, right now, before I do anything else. I was not at all sure myself that my friend Wau-Kok was the right one to be the chief of the clan. My idea of a chief was a man who could know his own mind surely, and then get done what needed to be done. I had blamed the long being with the old crippled chief for that, for Wau-Kok's indecision, and general mixing things all up. I was thinking that any other man of the clan would have been a better choice for that position. I was thinking that, maybe, we should not have split off from the other part of the clan.

After we had moved to a better place, not very far from the great canyon, I myself went to the rim of the great wound in Mother-Ground, and kept vigil there. That time I did not go down into any period of deep-vastation. (Years before that time, after I had first taken up my good place as a married man of the clan, I had done that.) That time, at the rim of the great canyon, I kept my vigil. I was wiser than I had been before, when I had done my vigil of my period of deep-vastation. I was one much needed in the new place where we were to try to pass the winter, so I did not go without food, that vigil. With me, by that time of my life, that was not necessary. Of course I ate only a little each day. (It would not do for me to get weak - enemies might come.)

I soon got into the good vigil-way-of-your-mind. Let me try to tell you about that. Of course you like the wise understanding invisible friend, Nature. If you have got so you are friending with him daily as a regular thing, there are times, good deeply happy times, when he comes right into your own too-small heart. You actually feel him there.

1863

How strange that experience is. It is as though the big person had purposely made himself small, so that he could crowd into that too small place, and be there awhile. You have the actual feeling of that in your heart. You feel that you have him in your own physical body, in your own heart. You are much surprised, the first time that happens to you. You are in no good feeling about that, for you know how much too small you are in all ways for the being in you of the great one. You wonder at that. You are very grateful, of course. You did not know, before that time, that the great Ko-Waa was like that. You have learned something new about the great invisible Father. That father is not so much like your human father as, maybe, you had thought he was; he is not as frequent a comer to you as the invisible Mother is. That coming into your heart, his coming, is different from the coming of Mo-Kaa to you. When she, the great invisible Mother, comes into your heart, you feel a glowing there. Much more frequently you feel that. You feel that that is more ordinary; you are more used to it.

I wish I could do what I once did, very many thousands of years ago. I had had the great father come to me so much that I was, in a way, familiar with him. Ordinarily you are more familiar with the "woman-side" of the great invisible friend. That time, that hard cycle of my life, I had great urgent need for power, so that I could carry through to a good end a very-secret movement among many thousands of slaves. I was so that I almost never had the one Mo-Kaa come to me. I was so much in need of Ko-Waa, the strong stern "manside" of the invisible friend, that I was not enough in the presence of the softer more kindly more inward side. Now, too, in these terrible times, I need to get back to where I was, in that slavery-cycle of my life. I will try to get to making more use of the "Ko-Waa" side of the great all-round friend. Of course there will be times when I will be in the inner home feeling that Mo-Kaa makes you feel, when she is there with you. If you only knew, you who read these lines, how very deeply good it is to know the friend as he actually is, so that he is to you as real as your intimate chum is (if you are fortunate enough to have

1864

one), you would be eager to get to know him yourself. I was thinking, in the night last night, about some of things I would need to put into this day's writing. I am this way: I write as long as my mind will let me do that, each day. I am told definitely what to do. There is no hazy foggy feeling about this work that I do. I am told what to do. I am even told just when to get up each morning. I am no slave. I am not being "bossed" by Still-voice. Still-voice and I are intimate friends. We work things out together in the friendly way that, normally, the wife and husband have. If you could get so you were working all your things out along with Ko-Waa and Mo-Kaa day after day, year after year, cycle-of-life after cycle-of-life - then you would be in practical heavenly life all the time. Get it into your head that no good idea ever became current in human history unless that thing actually was long ago, among thousands of people. I have to keep telling you some things over again. You are so much like I was, not many decades ago, this cycle of my life, that you need all this repetition. That old idea "heaven" means living in friendliness with invisible Nature, the person. That is all it means. But, do not get the idea that is not much. You know almost nothing of invisible Nature - the person. You, like almost everybody else, believe that what is called nature (with a small "n"), is only some "laws of nature" that some human thinkers discovered. You have the universal idea that "nature must be improved upon" by human workers, improved upon very much, can be improved upon very much, should be improved upon very much". You see what I mean. Only with the less-deep mind do the people who are now living cycles of the long-lives of them do their thinking, and planning and doing. I am in too much good feeling for all my friends, the human ones, to think to be blaming any person very much. The people of Japan, for instance - how can they know but what the things they were born into and grew up with are right - and all other kinds of people wrong?

Once, in that long-ago cycle of my life when I was trying to get a secret movement to doing the secret work among the wise slaves, so that, at a given definite time, there

1865

could be a universal uprising of all the many thousands of slaves, we had good use of our deep minds. We are not out for the least bit of revenge. What killing there would be would be only what was required to let all the slaves go away to freedom. We were able to do all that, a thing that had a very secret organization. Only those slaves who would go to the much trouble to learn the writing that the Yellow-legs people knew how to do could belong to that organization. It was Ko-Waa, not Mo-Kaa, who was with me, all those very hard years. I had come to know the invisible friend only after I had been taken and tattooed and trained as one of the lowest kind of slaves: I was not, before that time, knowing that there was any understanding invisible friend; (my mother had not known anything about that, nor my father). I have to go into all this, a little, for unless you know about some of these things, you will not be able to feel what my story means; it will be merely "words" in your ears. I am only one of the lowly people, talking to you, whoever you are. We human people are all lowly people. (What makes some human persons seem to many to be something more than lowly ones - it is not actually theirs; it belongs to the many people in their own small communities. Kings are such only because all that extra honor and glory and power was forcibly wrested away from the lowly people, long ago. Customs, as the generations pass, make it seem that great wrongs are good.) I have to do much writing that may seem to be out in the fringe of what the main story is about. It is out there. I had that "fringe" to the mind of me, while I was living my way, day after day, through the story I am telling to you. Can you not see that I must, somehow, give you some of the feelings that came, and went, that time, in my own mind? I cannot just "word" things right along in a kind of a narrow roadway; I must carry the whole scene along with me, and you, as we go together in this story. Because you who are listening to the story do not have anything of the full background that I, the teller of the story have, I must do this story as I am doing it. You will find that my deep mind knows what it is about. You will find that great Ko-Waa has worked together with

1866

me, and with my wife, in all this.

In one small thing I will say what you may believe is not true: "The great things of human life are out in the fine delicate fringes of your own best feelings."

I must say to you a good thing William Wordsworth once wrote, in one of his pieces of writing: "These beautious forms, through a long absence have not been to me as is a landscape to a blind man's eye: But oft, in lonely rooms, and 'mid the din of towns and cities, I have owed to them, in hours of weariness, sensations sweet, felt in the blood, and felt along the heart; and passing even into my purer mind, with tranquil restoration. Feelings too of unremembered pleasure - such perhaps as have no slight or trivial influence on that best portion of a good man's life, his little, nameless, unremembered acts of kindness and of love. Nor less, I trust, to them I may have owed another gift, of aspect more sublime, that blessed mood in which the burden of the mystery - in which the heavy and the weary weight of all this unintelligible world is lightened - that serene and blessed mood in which the affections gently lead us on - until (the breath of this corporeal frame and even the motion of our human blood almost suspended), we are laid asleep in body, and become a living soul - while with the eye made quiet by the power of harmony, and the deep power of joy, we see into the life of things."

What I wrote in the short paragraph preceding this one, made me think of all that I have quoted. We live in the deep mind, if we are actually "living". There is a psychologic region that lies between the less-deep mind and the deep mind. In the morning, when you have hardly waked up from sleep, you are in that region. You are in the state of mind and feeling that makes it possible to see either way, see back down into the things your submental mind had been doing while you were sleeping. And you are, in a way, aware of what is going on around you. I was thinking again of that thing Dickens wrote, about "the drowsy state between sleeping and waking" - when you see visions, and hear strange things. It is a very important fact he had discovered. Dickens was one who was a thinker. You should make the

1867

distinction between deep thinkers and mere writers. I keep thinking about the book, Forever Amber. I am wondering how it is that a mere writer easily gets the chance to say out to many millions of people what she wants to say, crude bawdy things, not any of it literature, while many deep thinkers (who have anxiously worked many years to try to think the continuing troubles of the whole human race all the way through to satisfying conclusions, so that the right way of doing may be got started), cannot get anything at all out to the people.

I was thinking, yet again, about what the people have to put up with all over the earth, what I have called "producer-management". We need to be getting to good clearness in our own minds about the terrible things that make it impossible for permanent peace to be in the earth. People are hopeless about war; they think another war is sure to come. They can see how the leaders of the people, the rulers of the big nations, are not going deep enough in their own thinking, harrassed as they continually are with many complicated problems, problems that have to be hastily settled in some way, so that other very important matters involving many millions of people may be gone into. People just seem to be able to "keep their heads above water", in the terrible earth-wide "flood" of bad conditions all over the earth.

How is it that by now, in the history of human peoples, we have it not nearly as good as the clans-people Indians had it, many thousands of years ago? Are we paid for all our continuing internal bad feelings, the bad muss the inner-lives of all of us are in, by such mere external things as radios, and cigarettes and airplanes and automobiles and new products chemistry gives us? We live, if we do actually "live", in the inner-life. Many millions of people, this era, have no, or very little, inner-life. A few bottles of beer, plenty of cigarettes, a woman who is as loose in sexual-matters as the man is himself - that is the "inner-life" of many millions of people, now in these times. A shortage of beer, or cigarettes, is a real calamity to them. Inner-life should mean, of course, the use of the deep mind. It is too much to expect people who have lived many cycles of their lives merely in the less-deep mind of them to take off suddenly, and get up into the deeper purer mind. The thing cannot be done quickly. You have to go through what may be, in your case, a terrible long-drawn-out mind-cleansing experience. I was wanting to get you to feel how things are, when the whole situation is all mixed up. I cannot do that easily. I might "tell" you that. I am now getting you mixed up in your own mind by the things I am writing, in this book. That thing is good. You are probably put out at me, for not going right along with the story. How could you be feeling what those Indians were feeling, if you yourself were in no mixed-up mood? Another thing, it is my deep mind that does this writing. I must not reason things out. I cannot write that way.

If you will think of the worst desert you know about, and put some dry scraggly bushes there, some clumps of them, and then put there the deepest great wide long funny queer palisaded mile-deep canyon - you will have some kind of a picture of how I was, in my mind, that time. I hated deserts. It was not only that bad desert, devastation, I had to face, that time, but the very much worse one that the great deep long ten-mile wide wound in old Mother-Ground was. See how that was, that time. I was the young minstrel of the small clan. It was the thing the invisible friend had put upon me. I had got back much from the preceding cycle of my life, so I knew that doing the work of a minstrel was my kind of work, in the long-life of me. We had had to migrate. I had been down, all those years. I had been by no means a minstrel the years of our wandering in deserts. (Worry, long-continued, is bad; you cannot have good use of the deep mind of you, if that has to be.) In no good feeling I had gone there to do that vigil.

It was a place from which I could look off down into the great deep wide palisaded canyon. My eyes were on that, as I was in my vigil. It changes. Each hour of the day it looks somewhat different. So deep it is, and so far can you look into it, that the distance purples things; that great canyon is "purple-deep". I was wondering why he, great Ko-Waa, had brought the remnant of the clan all the long way back to

1869

that region. (Remember, that same clan, in a former cycle of life, had had to migrate from that region, right after the great terrible devastation had been done by that big flood.) I was in my vigil. It happened. It was what I needed at that time. I had wanted to know how it was that such terrible things had been permitted to happen to our small clan those years. As minstrel I needed to be clear about all that. It was this way. I was keeping great Ko-Waa in my mind. (That is the thing you try to do all during deepvastation. It is not enough to have him in your heart, you must yourself do the work of keeping him in your own deep mind. It is only there that you can come to know how he is, and what he is thinking. You need to know what he thinks about the great thing that you have not been able to get good clearness about. It has to be great enough to you, a thing important enough, so that you go alone to some hidden place where you can be for many days undisturbed, and just "have it out" with him, the great invisible Father. He it is, not Mo-Kaa, who takes care of all that. It takes the stern just father to do that. He has to be terrible to you, at times. You may even have to go down into the worst state any person ever has to go into. You are one of his children. He is, of course, not any kind of a GOD. To think that about him is a kind of an insult to him. He is like a wise understanding human father. He is that way to human persons. To ants, he is like a wise understanding one of those small people.

It came to me. After only a few days, that time, my thing came to me. It was this way. My mind was on the great invisible Ko-Waa. I was thinking steadily. It is not hard for a minstrel to do that. Into my mind, along with being passive in the presence of Ko-Waa came my thing, the thing that I was needing at that time. It was as though I was let see what was in the mind of invisible great Ko-Waa. What my eyes were then looking at was "the sign". It came to me that the very great deep wound in old Mother-Ground was my thing. It was as though my eyes had but opened - and that was there. The "sign" it was, the fact that it was my message, came to me. My vigil had given

1870

me my message. How great that was! I thought about it awhile. It was as though the invisible friend let me know how he himself was feeling about that great bad thing he had had to permit, many decades before that time. He too was there, with me, thinking sadly about that. It was as though he had had me come all the very long way there, to be with him, again, that cycle of my life, in that place, so as to consider that thing. You could not possibly put the titanic human thing into any words. You had to, somehow, represent that thing - so that the two minds, his and mine, might be on the same great thought. Mile-deep, ten miles wide, very many miles long, that same "sign" is still there. True, it is not as bad a thing to look at now as it was that time very many centuries ago. A sign cut a mile deep in rock - that is something to think of. I leave that with you, whoever you are who is now reading this. It is a fact. You can go there yourself, and look down into it. Maybe, it might possibly be, invisible Ko-Waa too will be there, with you, as you do your sad looking. Maybe that would do you good.

Vastation is not enough. Many millions of people are being vastated by the things the nations are compelled to live through now in these times. Will that degree of vastation make "changed" persons of them? Will Winston Churchill be a "changed" person because of the pressure he has had to bear for years? I wish it could be that only that much vastation was all that would be necessary to get the human race up out of the age-old HELL it is down in. It is actual terrible HELL. We all have to continually live down in HELL. Only deep vastation, in the deep minds of some millions of thinkers, can make a sure beginning at getting the whole human family back into the ancient clan-way of living. No amount of propaganda for yet more "social-reform" will do any good. The recorded history of the human peoples is one long heart-rending record of "reforms" that failed. The Big-Business way of managing everything for all the people everywhere is what keeps us all working as slaves at jobs. "Make things good for Business - and all will be good for all people everywhere,"

1871

is how more and more millions of people have come to believe. "The deep mind? What is that? What are you giving us anyway? Who are you - some new kind of a crank?"

In about ten years, we were like a good normal clan. We were small. That was good. Each one of us knew, and liked, all the others of the clan. Young Wau-Kok had gone through a great change. Deep vastation had made "a changed person" of him. He was now the wise careful quiet-minded hearkening chief. He was, in a way, the young acting-chief to old wise talk-less Soo-Maa-Hillo.

What happened that time at Pointingfingerrock, that thing the young minstrel Ki-Mo-Go told us about, my wife and me, was a thing that happened to Wau-Kok and his family. That was one of the stories of our clan. They had not jumped to their death, as the old man had thought, at that time. They had seen that there was an easy way to get out of the bad fix they were in. A split came several times in the thin water of the great falls, there at that place at the end of Pointingfingerrock. Through that they all saw what to do, jump through the thin sheet of water down into a deep pool that was behind the falls at that place. Up out of that pool they could easily get, up on to the higher level from which the great falls plunged. All that is in my mind, as I write. A number of times I have written that out, in good order. It is a good interesting story. I must leave all that out. It has to be a short book. I am wanting to do some much-needed work, to try to get thinkers to themselves get things back from past cycles of their own lives, many centuries ago. My way is to tell stories from far back there. Take them, or have nothing to do with them.

In my mind is a good small old story. It will fit in well here. "Be in your own small world," my good mother said. "How important you seem to think you are. If it is a thing that big, then the chief should attend to it, or the old minstrel." My thought, that time, after she had said that to me, was this: "You are woman. What do women know about such things?" Of course I made no words even in my mind, that time; that was a thing that was always all in the air, in our settlement. Women were,

1872

of course, that way, not thinking that boys could ever do any of the big things. It was my own idea. Why had the chief not done that thing long before? "Any one could see that would be a good thing. The thing should have been done - cut deeper the ditch that would drain a bad swamp that was always a nuisance to all of us." I would be no mere woman-boy, not anything like that. It would do no harm to go work at that thing myself, in secret. I was not let do that thing. As things were, at that time, it would have been bad for our safety, if no bad swamp had been there. Of course a small Indian boy was not with his mind out all over the great region - many warring clans. I was in my sleep that very next night. (I had it all decided that I would go alone to make a start at the big work. Early next morning, I would sneak away from my home, to be gone all day.) I came up out of sleep. Right there before me was a savage fierce Indian, with a long keen flint-knife, ready to kill me. I was knowing right away that that was a vision-thing. I was used to things like that. It showed me clearly why our wise chief had not drained the big swamp. Ko-Waa, that invisible chief, did that to me.

A brown face slowly pushed itself through the bush. No sound came. The Indian had been there very still, motionless, for a long time. No danger-sign had come. The woods were dry. No slight wind stirred them. How noiseless it was in those woods, as if no thing ever moved there, as if for centuries no thing had moved there. It was not a good feeling those woods gave that lone Indian. "They seem to be waiting," that Indian thought to himself. "They seem to have been waiting for many years." (He had scouted that whole sunken little wooded valley. No signs of Indians having been there had he found.) Again he was at the edge of the deep little gorge. How good that little cool gorge was. He had not yet got down to that good clear stream that was in the gorge. (What water he had needed, plenty of it, he had got from a spring that was in a low place of the sunken valley, not very far from the queer end of the long desert ridge that, coming far across the desert, had decided to stop there in that wooded sunken

1873

valley.) The lone Indian was again near to the little gorge, near to the side of it. He had already scouted all along the other side of the gorge. He had seen where a big groove, down near the water, had been cut deep into the rock, in places where the current had been strong, some time of high water. He had thought that some Indians might be camped down in that gorge. (It did not seem possible that such a good pagus could be unoccupied.) He looked very carefully through the bush for any sign of any Indian. He had looked in all the places, down in the gorge, that could have been used for a camp-place, all the places that he could see from the other side of the gorge. He had nearly finished the scouting of both sides of the gorge. This time too he saw no sign of any Indian. He went back into the woods from that place.

The big Indian went back to the big spring. It was near sunset when he got there. He must go thank Sun for guiding him to that good place. Now that he was sure that place was an unoccupied place, so that they could have it for their own pagus, he must go thank Sun for that. He washed himself all over in the water of that big spring. He had a gourd with him in his pack. With that he poured water all over himself. He went, all wet, on the way to go up to the top of the high end of the queer ridge. It was high up there. From there he would thank old Sun for giving him the necessary guidance, so that he had found that good place.

About one moon later, a clan of brown-haired Indians came and slid down (like a clan of apes), into the little deep gorge, slid down a long vine-cable - eager to get down to the big stream of clear water. Each one had some kind of a pack on, even the children. Some of those packs were occupied baby-baskets (what a lark for that chubby hairy brown naked Indian-boy - looking out upon all that, with wise age-old Indian eyes).

Chief Wau-Kok had not told them a thing about what he had found; he had not been permitted by the invisible friend to do that. He told them, when he had got back from that hard scouting-journey, that he had found a place that would do for them. They had it hard that time, going all that long

1874

way with their heavy packs to that far-away place that their chief had found. They had put packs on some of their goats. Everybody carried what was for him, or her, a heavy pack; even the young children carried something. They had cached all of their things and their stored food that they could not take that first trip to their new home-region.

It was the driest region those Indians had ever gone into. The farther east from their former home-region they went, the drier it was. "The Chief does not stop this day to rest in the middle part of the day," said a little husky-voiced thirsty Indian-boy to his little sister, "because he has to get us to the next spring, before it gets too dark to find it." Not a drop had there been in any one of their big water-bags for two days. They had had to get along on chewed cactus. That day there had been no cactus. Those Indians did not ever have any idea of complaining about things like that. (We in these times are people who have been "taken care of" for so many cycles of our lives, that we have got into the habit of thinking someone is to blame if we are not as comfortable as we think we ought to be. In those times, very far back in the history of the human race, people were more like what the Eskimos are - in that matter; they took what the situation gave them. They saw first what was good. If there was a hard situation - then there was challenge in it; - "who would like to have things easy all the time?" Danger was a thing they continually had to have in the back of the mind. It made for a quiet mastery of whatever it was the day's situation put upon you.)

Evening was coming on, and they had not got to the spring. (The Chief had not said that they would come to a spring that day; but the Indian children had felt that they would get to a spring that day.) They had been looking for many hours far ahead on the dry barren desert to a long rocky ridge that lay stretched for many miles across that desert region. Those Indians had thought that the Chief had found a place for their home over on the other side of that ridge. At long last they had got to that ridge. They had expected that they would go up over that ridge. The Chief

1875

did not go up on that ridge; he led the way along the base of it. They were driving their thirsty goats ahead of them as they went. The scouts were in charge of these tired thirsty goats. They went for a while along the base of that ridge. They came to rising ground. Wearily the tired thirsty goats went slowly up the rise. The leader of those goats stopped, and stared, when she got to the top rise. Immediately a scout went quickly there, his bow ready. He crouched down, as he got near. He went flat. Another scout went quickly there. The clan of Indians, seeing that, disappeared from sight. (It was a barren place. You would not have noticed any of those Indians there, if you had not seen them go into hiding. You know about camouflage. Indians practised that very far back in ancient times. You would not have known an Indian was anywhere near - unless you felt the jeopardy-sign. Young Indian-boys were good at that. That was instinctive with them; they seemed to know just the right place, and just the right adjustments of their parts - so as to blend themselves in with that place they had quickly, instinctively, chosen.) The chief was hidden up near where those scouts were hidden. Presently Indians stood up and signalled the clan to come on. When they got to the top of that little rise, they stopped in astonishment. Trees! a whole long sunken valley full of big trees - trees to wander about in for miles - and, they knew water was there. They went on, cautiously.

Soon there were campfires going, there in the woods, near the big spring that was in a hollow.

The chief told them, that evening, what that place was, the old home-region of their clan. Barren deserts stretched all around that hidden oasis. The stream ran down in a gorge, so that when you looked across that stretch of desert, you did not know any stream was there. That long desert ridge had its high abrupt end there in that sunken valley. How good it is, when you get home to your old home. When all those Indian-women knew that that was the old home of the clan, before the terrible flood had come, how great was the feeling of gratitude to great Mother, great invisible Mo-Kaa. They had been, they felt, wander-

1876

ing in bad places for many hard years. Now, at long last, they had got home. To Indian women what they like is to have a good settlement, where the families of the clan can have things in good order. "Family" and all matters connected with the family-life was women's work. "Clan" was more the work of the men.

You who now are reading this book must get out of your mind any thought of "Redskin" Indians. The Indians I am telling stories about were people who lived thousands of years before there were any of those kinds of Indians. We need to think "Settlement Indians" when we think of the ancient Indians. They were not ever without a good settlement for their clan to have the permanent home in. How good that was. I was interested, not many months ago, to see how, even now, some Indians look upon the place that is "Indian-reservation" to them. "Have you been out home lately?" one Indian woman who had her work in the small city we live in said, to an Indian friend. "I am going to take a good rest," another Indian woman said, at another time; "I am going out home for a while." I heard things like that. Even now, after all the many years of being "overwhelmed" with "White-people" ways of doing, the Indian women think, with good liking, of their own old Indian ways of living, out in a wild natural region where only Indians are let have homes. Have White people any such real home (clan-home) to go to? How homesick I often am for a home-settlement such as I had, very long ago, when I was a member of a clan of ancient-Indians.

How early the Indian-children got up, that next morning "Our fine new pagus. The one the clan used to have very long ago." What goings off, in the dim light of very early morning, on little exploring expeditions. The woods got a good surprise, that memorable morning. How long they had been waiting for that.

" 'Y! we forgot to look to Sun, this morning. I will go me quick back up on to the desert, up there, and do my honor to him now." Three little Indian boys ran so very quickly that you hardly saw them as they passed by you. Out a way up on the higher place they stopped, and looked

1877

up to old Sun. The thing was to see which one could do it first. Each one of the three small Indian boys tried to be first, in doing that thing, look the blaze of Sun away, so as to see the blue of him.

One boy stood there long, that morning. The running of the two others away from there did not get him to go. He had trouble in his mind, that morning. He had made a mistake - had not done the thing he had as his morning work. Because this was such a good new wonderful interesting wooded place, (not dry desert all about as far as the eyes could take your mind), he had been too hasty in his doing up his part of the camp work, so that his mother had noticed, and had called him back. He had not packed his things up in his own pack. His mother had tried to get him to come back. He had not gone back when his mother had called after him. That had not been right to great invisible Mo-Kaa. So, now, when he was alone there (his two friends having run back down into the woods), he went all out, deep in his mind, to great Mo-Kaa.

A thing happened, soon after that, a sign given to him alone. A small sign, that one. He had but looked down from looking up long into the deep blue of old Sun, so his eyes were not as sharp as usually they were. What that young Indian boy saw was one tiny "track" in a place of fine dust. (Tracks - that was what that Indian boy was liking. He was one Indian boy who liked the "wild" of wild animals. He was Waa-Ho, the small boy of the big chief.) "I will go me down," he said. "I will see me. May it not be my big sick brother would like him to come with me this morning, this very different morning, to tell me what this very - it moves!" Waa-Ho looked at that one small "track". It was, he saw, not a track at all. He did not know what it was. It moved, moved very slowly. "It's a sign," he knew in the quiet of his mind. "The slow moving of it is some kind of a sign to me." Wondering about that, he went walking, did not run. When he got to their camp, he saw that some move was about to be made. All the small packs were being put on. (The regular order of the Indian camp was there, complete. Not a thing was out of place. No

1878

"taming" of that place, that wild place, had been made, by the coming there of those wild Indians.) One thing was not quite right. Waa-Ho, seeing that, felt ashamed. His things were where he had left them, when he had gone off with the other boys. He went to packing up his things. He took plenty of time to do that. He would not go with the others; that would be a kind of punishment he would make himself take, for being careless.

(It was not an unusual thing, in those times, for even a young child to be thinking serious thoughts about how he himself should be doing. Of course the child knew that his work was not very important, that doing of necessary camp-work, but he knew that if he let himself be careless day after day with his not-interesting home duties, then his mind would not be right for things that a scout has to do. All Indian boys had to do very rigid strict strenuous scout training for many years.)

All the other Indians were there, at the place where they would go down into the deep gorge, when little Indian boy, Waa-Ho, got in sight of them. He was not thinking then, of any need to go slow. He saw, from a distance, how they would go down. He saw that the chief, his father, was just going down out of sight, going down the little pine tree that grew out from the side of the gorge, and then up, so that it reached up above the top of the rocks. Waa-Ho saw, as he was running fast to get there, that you had to slide down a steep place, be very sure to catch hold of the little pine tree, climb down the little pine, and then go the long way down into the deep narrow gorge, by going down a long one of the twisted tough vines, a big one that had grown up from below. (That one had out-grown them all. It had reached all the way to the base of the little pine, and was all securely grown all about it.) Getting there late, little Waa-Ho had not seen that good order was to be, during that going-down. Water, deep running water was down in that good-smelling deep little gorge. All the people, he thought were wanting much to get down there quick. So, being a boy, and being the young son of the chief of the clan, he ran right to that steep little place you had to slide down, and down he slid, to the

1879

little tree. Of course that sent a small shower of small pieces of broken rock down over the edge of the gorge there. The chief, only a little way down below, looked up, and saw who it was. He was ashamed. "'You climb back up, and wait till I tell you to come down."

How shamed the little Indian boy felt; he had been blamed by the chief, in the presence of the whole clan.

They all stood there, those many Indians. A while they let that small Indian boy be rebuked by that thing that he had done. Then, speaking sternly, the chief said: "Go Now!"

In deep shame Waa-Ho went down. His day, that first day in that wonderful place, he had spoiled. He was much more in shame when it came to him that he had not made use of the good little sign that the small slow-moving thing was, of that little thing, up on the desert, that small thing that at first he had thought was some kind of a tiny track.

When Waa-Ho got all the way down the big twisted strong living rope, he saw what to do. How that was a wonder place. He got slowly off the vine-cable, big and twisted of three separated vines (big there at the lower part of it). Waa-Ho had taken in how that vine was rooted down below in the small beach that was there at that place like a long narrow lake. His mind took in all that, as he was getting slowly off from that rope made by the twisted living tough vines, on to the rock floor of a strange squared groove in the rock. (He had seen those two big grooves down in the bottom of the gorge, one each side of it, near the water; he had seen that from above, when at dawn he had gone to take an early morning look down, to see that deep clear water.)

Shame, deep shame, in him in the near presence alone of the chief, he went from that place, went slowly away from his father, the chief. He felt better when he had got out of sight of that place where the clan would come down. He knew that he would keep out of sight of any one of them all that day.

"Coon-tracks!" he said to himself, as he saw a small part of a fresh coon-track where a little wet on the rock of the rock-floor of that big groove had let part of the foot of a coon leave its mark. That was what Waa-Ho liked. Tracks of wild animals were to him something like the scent of a

1880

wild animal is, to a trained dog. The Indian boy went on the trail of that coon.

Up on top, where all the Indians were waiting to go down, a time of some uncertainty was. Little Waa-Ho had gone down. Of course the family of the chief should go down next after the chief. (The scout would send them down by families.) Taa-Laa-Go? What about listless Taa-Laa-Go? The scout felt not to tell Taa-Laa-Go to go down that dangerous place, he being in the listless condition he was in. (He had seemed to be not very listless that morning: he had taken interest in that good gorge. He had stood long, looking down at the several rapids that could be seen, down there, as you stood on that high place.) Wish-Naa-Gaa knew that it was for her to manage her sick son. She had, of course, lifted that matter up to invisible Mo-Kaa. A flight of small birds flying over, high up in the air just then caught her eyes. She looked up and saw a singular thing: two of those small flying birds were a little different from all the other ones of that flock. Light-breasts those two had. One of the two flew, in the formation they were all flying in, a little ahead of the other light-breasted one. She knew that for a sign. She knew what to do. She was to go down, and Taa-Laa-Go would follow her. She slid down the little steep place, and went down. Taa-Laa-Go slid down next. He was not listless then. He seemed something like his own former self.

How good that made all those Indians feel. (Taa-Laa-Go was to every Indian of the clan one who was a different kind of an Indian; you felt that. You did not have to get to like him, you liked him already as soon as you saw him for the first time. And you kept on feeling that way; it did not seem to wear off from knowing him a long time. It had been something of a personal calamity to each person when sickness had come to him. Each person felt a distinct loss. The clan seemed - to be waiting to become its old happy self. The children missed him, in a way, more than did the older Indians. He knew how to make children, girls and boys alike, be happy in some kind of a new game-thing, that, all of a sudden, would come up out of his mind. He would be sometimes very stern and strict with the younger

1881

children, and then he would be his "laugh-self". He would make the queer talk that you were supposed to believe came out the mouth of one of the tree-faces, calling far across, in the twilight, to other queer tree-faces.)

That day gave Wish-Naa-Gaa and Wau-Kok good hope that Taa-Laa-Go would again get back to be like his former good self, in the clan.

The chief-scout thought to send them down by families. Of course after Taa-Laa-Go had gone down, his sister Ki-Maa-Ni went down. "You next," Waa-Ste said, looking to the oldest person in the clan. Soo-Maa-Hillo, (the old Indian woman who did not talk), did not keep anyone waiting; thought she was very old, she was as quick as the quickest one of the clan.

"You next," Waa-Ste called, looking to Saar-Tam-Mo. Big bulky Saar-Tam-Mo was shy; he made one little motion with one hand. Waa-Ste understood; "the many children should go down before the older ones." Waa-Ste saw that he was being too formal. "All the children line up," he said.

Children came from among the older ones. They were to be the honored ones, that time. Waa-Ste put each one down the slide-place, as they came there to him. He saw that they could do it without any being anxious about it. He was facing toward the tree. The many Indian children went down, each one with some kind of a small pack.

The chief-scout looked each side of him. No more children came. So he called to the oldest man to go down. That old man slid down. Then, a thing happened. "Daddy," (the Indian word that meant that) Waa-Ste heard that behind him. He turned. He saw that his own little undersized shy girl was there. (She had not gone down with the other children.) Waa-Ste knew how shy she was. He would have gone down with her, all the way down, for she was very precious to him. (She had been born before the normal time, and they had had trouble getting her to live. So, she being not like the other children of that family, they had favored her much, loving her the more, because of her small size.) She was as sure of herself as was any of the other children.

1882

Waa-Ste looked at the small mite of a girl, as she slid fast down the little steep place. He was not without anxiety when he saw that she used only one hand to catch hold of the tree. How well she managed. She had on what for her was too big a pack. The pack had slipped, a little, as she had slipped quickly down the slide. With one hand, she pushed back her pack, while with the other she caught hold of a small branch of the pine tree. That gave her father an anxious moment. (I must tell you an interesting thing; stop the story a moment. This cycle of my life, years ago, at a time when I was working at this part of the story I was trying to write out, a strange thing happened to me. I had been asleep. In the early morning, there came to me two precious "Daddy's". How strangely that affected me. There was a feeling of "preciousness" about that. I could not but know that that had been spoken to me, some time, by a precious little child. All that day after that I could yet feel in my heart the preciousness of it. In a few days it came to me what that was. Thing after thing had been coming back to me, from out of that cycle of my life. I was getting along well with getting things from far back there. Not yet had it come to me who I was, which one of that clan I was. That happening showed me that I had been the father of that small Indian girl, for I saw at the time I heard those "Daddy's", that dangerous little slide-place.)

There were one hundred fifty-six Indians in the clan. It did not take them long to get down into the little gorge. What a day that day was, in the life of that clan. (You cannot know how good water is, unless you have yourself lived long in a dry hot treeless all-open-to-the-brassy-sky desert. No escape. You feel that. Each day will be like the day before. Only for a few months in the winter will it be different. The air is so dry that it drinks up every bit of moisture that is not "held on to", in some way. The small leaves of the desert plants and shrubs and taller bushes all have to "varnish" themselves with a good protecting coat of some substance that they have learned how to make, so as to keep within the leaves the moisture. Even if you water well plants that are from some moisture region, they

1883

cannot grow in that dry region. Only trees and plants that have an impervious coat to the leaves of them can do well there. How good it is, when you have been for maybe a year steadily far out in a desert, to go from that dry region. You know it, when you get near to the first place where any water is. How good to your eyes even some little willow tree is. How your whole self seems to feel a deep relief. And if it is a big clear stream of running water - you want to camp right there.) What a day they had, those many happy Indians. Of course they spent most of that day in the water. Taa-Laa-Go went, alone, all the long way up the gorge to the upper end of it, where you could see desert beyond. He did not get back till it was nearly dark, and savory smells were there in the wide place of one of the strange grooves in the gorge-wall. The camps of the families were there.

Waa-Ho, little Indian-boy Waa-Ho - what a day that was in his life. He was at what he liked to do, all that day. And he did some very important work for the clan, that day. No Indian had as yet found a good way to get down into the vertical-walled deep gorge. (Wau-Kok, when he had scouted there the first time, had not seen how to get down by a good way into the gorge. He had gone down by way of that strong vine-rope. He thought there was a good way down for of course he had seen the tracks of the coons that had been down there.) Little Waa-Ho it was who found the coon-way to get up.

"It is a thing I need to do first," said Waa-Ho to himself. "Not till I have done some good thing for the clan can I go have fun in the good cool water. I will not even go down the wall here in this good place to wet my foot in it. I will be hard with myself, and maybe I will remember to not do that kind of careless way any more. I did know that that slow-going of that small thing meant I myself must be on the watch, so as not to go fast at a wrong time. If I had not been running to get to the place when I saw that already they had begun to go down, of course I would have known to not jump down there then. I must put all that from me, behind my back, and look sharp all this day. What do I know but some big wild thing may try to get me, if I do not give my mind

1884

well to even the very small signs? I thought, at the first that that was one of the queer tracks the little-people make, that Laa-Go used to tell me about."

Had it not been for a thing that Waa-Ho believed was the doing of one of the fairies, he might have missed finding where the coons got up out of the gorge. It was one of the smallest kinds of feathers, a single tiny down feather. The Indian boy smelled strong the smell coon-people have to the bodies of them. Even if he had not seen any tracks, he would have known that coons had been there. It was only a very faint odor. Even some of the scouts might not have noticed that. (Waa-Ho was specially good at that.) He had gone nearly all the way across the little sunken valley down in the big groove that was there on one side of the bottom of the gorge. The place where the gorge made a square turn, to go on down the valley, was a place where the big groove was nearly filled with rocks that had caved down, from out a big fissure of the gorge-wall. Where the coons would go there, it was not an easy thing to know. Waa-Ho had a way of doing (when he was following any not easy to find trail of some animal), he would be very quiet, not only in all his body, but in his mind, as well. He had stood there a while, looking, and taking in all the smells, the very faint ones. He knew that not only coons would go there, but some other smaller kinds of animals. He was just about to go, try to see if he could see some hole in the pile of loose rocks, when he saw tiny very faint movement. He came alert. He looked there. He missed seeing what that was. "I think, could that be one of the little-people!" he said to himself, awe in him. (Many times he had watched long in some good place, to see if he could get to see the fairies. How many stories he knew of the strange wonderful doings and sayings of fairies.) He waited there awhile, more quiet in his mind because of the awe that was there. He soon saw what it was, a very fine very small feather. Some disappointment he felt, until it came to him that an invisible fairy might be what was making the feather go up a little way, and then let it float down again, behind some rocks that were there.

1885

In a little while he went there. He saw right away that he had happened onto the way by which the coons got up out of the gorge. It was a good hidden way. It was this way, back behind that pile of loose rocks; much water had rushed down a big fissure from above, and had cut out a channel in the floor of the big groove (the big groove Waa-Ho had come all that way there in.) The animals would go up over the pile of loose rocks, and would disappear up the wide fissure in the gorge-wall.

Much excited, the Indian boy went up the steep way. The bottom, smooth from water that, sometime years before, had gone down the place there, led steeply up. Though the fissure was narrow, it was wide enough for even big broad Saa-Tam-Mo to go in. The coon-way had a hidden upper end to it. Dense brush was there. (Waa-Ho did not then go out through that brush to see where the way had come out at, up on top. He was wanting to get down to that water. He had done the thing he had wanted to do for the clan.) Back down the steep way he went. Soon he was in the water.

In the afternoon of that day, Waa-Ho got to the lower end of the gorge. He went on down the stream, to see how the water would do, when it got out onto the desert. That day he did not find out. He saw that the stream went a way that was not easy to follow; the water spread out. Good green growth was there. It was a good place to be. (Waa-Ho was feeling bad because of what had happened that morning. He was lonely. He knew what fun all the other boys were having together.) In some loneliness the Indian boy lay down in the tall green growth that was in the place he had come to. He went to sleep. He slept a while. He was waked by a peculiar smell. He had never smelled any smell like that one before. What could it be? He was puzzled. He knew it was no smell of any animal, for there was too the smell of smoke. The odor was faint. He looked in the direction from which the small light wind had brought the smell to him. He thought he saw where faint smoke was. He went, to go see what that was. Fear was in him, for who but enemy-Indians would be there?

1886

What Waa-Ho saw, when he looked down from above that place, was the two Du-Saarte Indians of their clan, roasting some fish on a small fire. (Waa-Ho had never been told that the Indians who were of Du-Saarte's clan used fish for their eating. He had seen only the father of Ho-Pek, and Ho-Pek herself of the Du-Saarte Indians. He of course supposed all Indians were much like the ones of his own clan. He did not like Ta-Goomi and his Mate; but he thought that it was because they were of a different clan. He felt a strange dislike for them. He knew now that they were bad. He knew that they had come far from any of the others of the clan, so that what they were doing would not be found out. Waa-Ho knew, of course, that what they were doing was much against Nature; he felt disgust. Waa-Ho discovered that day for himself why his father, the chief, had frequently done the things chiefs had to do, go look, to make sure things are right in the places the families of the clan live in. Of course Wau-Kok had gone to all of the homes when they had lived in the canyon-settlement, so that Ta-Goomi would not know that he and his mate alone had to be watched. Wau-Kok had not wanted to take those two into the clan, of course. The young man and his mate had come with a story that old Du-Saarte had driven them out from his clan. Wau-Kok knew that they would be killed by the chief, if they went back down to their own clan. So, much against his liking, he had taken those two Indians in. He did not take them into the clan, but he permitted them to live in a home in the settlement of the clan. He had to show those two ignorant Indians many things. They knew nothing of the kind of life lived in families, for they had known no family life: in their clan no family life was (except the one good family that Ho-Pek's father had made). In permitting Ta-Goomi to do that, come live in their settlement, Wau-Kok had made those two Indians promise to live as the other Indians of that clan lived. Especially he made them promise to do no eating of any flesh of any kind. Of course that was very hard on those two for awhile for fish was the thing the Du-Saarte Indians ate most of, in that settlement where

1887

those two had been children. It was only by the careful watching by Wau-Kok, and some of the scouts, that those two Du-Saarte Indians were kept from trying to kill some small animals, rabbits, or kill birds. Ta-Goomi was too lazy to learn to do good work with a bow. He could spear fish. That was what he had liked to do. They were like two retarded children, trying to live adult life. They had no children: that young Indian woman knew how to prevent the having of children. They did not want to have any children. Ever since those two had come to the settlement to live, they had been a trouble to the clan. It was a difficult problem. There seemed to be no way to do that would be satisfying. All this will let you know how it was that those two Indians did not really belong in that clan. When they saw fish in the stream of the gorge, how they were glad. They were that simple in their minds that they thoguht they could separate from the clan, and live by themselves, somewhere in that pagus.

The story of what happened, after Waa-Ho had reported what he had seen to the chief, I got when Waa-Ho was a grown Indian. No story was told about any of that by the chief, or by Waa-Ho, at the time those two Du-Saarte did not come back. The clan did not know what had become of those two Du-Saarte Indians. The clan supposed that they had tried to go out on the desert along down the stream that flowed out from the lower end of the gorge on to the desert, and not being scouts, had got lost. No party was sent out, however. They knew that the chief knew things that he did not want to tell. A big bear was killed by the chief, about the time of the disappearance of those two Du-Saarte Indians. Some ones of the clan thought that maybe the two had been killed by that bear. People could not but be glad that those two were no longer in the clan. In those times, it was not done that strangers lived along year after year in any clan. If they could not be initiated into the clan then they could not continue to be there. The feelings of people took good care of that. Normally a person who did not belong in the clan would not stay there. Years after that thing had happened, when

1888

Waa-Ho was a grown Indian, he happened to tell me a thing that got him started to telling me the full story. I will not tell that story in this book. It is not one of the stories that would add anything useful to the clearing of the minds of people about the things that are important.

However "close" you may go to the necessary true normal way of living, you are unable to get to deep satisfaction in the long-life of you. No matter how many hundreds of cycles of life you live, you do not ever come to deeply satisfying living. "Closeness" to a right normal thing does not make you be more normal. You may be so very close to the normal way of living that no mind could see that there was any least separation between your way of living and the normal way of living, and yet your way will not be the normal way - and you will go on your way in the long-life of you to final doom. Do a thing now, you reader of this book. (Mind you, I am not implying that you are wrong and I am right; there is none of that in this that I am writing.) This is pure science that I am now writing. Look at an interesting matter of pure science. You will be interested in this. Go to Merriam's International Webster's dictionary, and look up the word "asymptote". Read what is said about that, and see what the diagrams mean. The two ways of living may even cross, as two straight lines cross; even at that crossing-place, where the small parts of the lines are seemingly "identical", the two ways of living are not the same.

Those two Du-Saarte Indians had been spared the fate the other Indians of their clan had met up with, a flood in the gorge of Great Canyon. They had been given the opportunity of living in a good clan, in which life was normal. Had they been willing to learn to think deeply they could have become useful members of that clan. Deep thinking is what will get the millions of people who will resolutely and continuously think deeply about problems of human living up out of the HELL we are now living in, and will do away with that HELL. Some deep thinking is now being done by many millions of persons. The terrible anguish the millions of people have had to live in, since

1889

this last very terrible war got going at its worst, has done that good thing, made millions of persons think deeply, get out of their complacency and do some deep thinking for themselves. Already one who himself thinks deeply can see symptoms of a change in the way many people are thinking. I was heartened to read only yesterday a little thing that said that the way known as "competition" is dead. We need to know that that word stands for big business "profits". We need to know that those kinds of "profits" mean graft. The affairs of the whole human race have been secretly managed for thousands of years by a relatively few "influential" persons of great wealth - for selfish purposes of great graft, or for fostering some form of centralization of government. Those two things, great graft and centralization of government, are what thinking persons should think into. (I will not say what I have thought out, about all that. Each person for himself must get to the place where he sees the important matters of human life, not merely with the present cycle of life in his view, but with whole long reaches of the long-life in his view.)

We had got to a new interesting wild pagus. It was ours. It was safe from the danger of being raided by war-liking Indians. We were not in any haste to be doing anything about getting settled there. "Be Ko No Gau Tai" was an old saying with us. "Be not too ready to do". We liked to think and feel. We had done a good thing, had made a good change in the location of our settlement. For our needs this desert "oasis" was better than the safe place we had had, down a little way in the great canyon. We would go on little exploring jaunts in our woods. How good it was to have woods, woods to wander in, even "get lost" in - for a little while. New places you had not yet been in, to see. New plants to wonder at. How much the Indian children got out of that good change from the former pagus to the new one. How much more thinking they did, than if they had remained in good comfort in the old loved homes. How good old loved homes are. All children should be born in some good old loved home, and grow up in it till he, or she, is at least three years old. Then maybe a journey to some very dif-

1890

ferent kind of region where the people speak a foreign language would be a good deep change. How can a young child get to thinking deep thoughts about human ways of living, unless he, or she, actually lives a while where no words he, or she, understands are ever heard? I think that the present-time custom of waiting till after the young person is through college before he is given the chance to go abroad is all wrong. How much better it would be if the children had that deepening of their minds before they had to start in at the long years of schooling they have to go through. I am not at all liking the way the schools are managed in these times. I think back to the very ancient times. One thing stands out very clearly in my mind. Deep-thinking was fostered by the ancient clan-way of growing children, culturing them. Deep-thinking is not fostered by the very expensive schools of the white-people. What more is there to say about this very important matter?

As we got organized (each family in the camp the father and mother had chosen), homes began to grow. Some of the homes grew in good places down in the gorge. What a refuge from the bad desert that good cool moist fragrant pretty gorge was. How we Indians did love our gorge. No other clan of Indians we knew about had as good a pagus as our pagus was. Come in from a two-month hard journey very far out in the dry hot terrible dangerous desert. Go down into the cool moist fragrance of that! Only persons who know desert-life can have any clear ideas about how you feel deep in you, at a time like that. How you are grateful to great Mo-Kaa and great Ko-Waa. You have that to think back to, as you set out on a long hard desert journey, and that to look forward to, as you come your weary hard way back.

How can I ever be grateful enough to DESERT? DESERT is to me like a very wise old understanding "Indian friend". How very terrible was the continuing unescapable anguish of those years, this cycle of my life. (I will not tell you definitely that private matter.) But for some periods of living far out on a desert, I would have wrecked this cycle of my life. How good it was when my work on the desert would

1891

permit me to go off far from any human place, and just be there alone a while. How still it was. How wise and old and "INDIAN" all things seemed. No "modern-conveniences" anywhere. The small wild lone desert bird, who had her nest down a good distance in an old abandoned mineshaft, so as to have it cool, and safe from snakes - how often my mind has gone back to that. How I liked the "scraggy elbows" of the low branches of the old desert-tried wise moisture-hoarding cresote-bushes, "elbows" that called attention to themselves by the short parts of circles they had cut in the ground, when kept in motion forth and back by continuing desert winds. The farness wildness of all that, the all-open-to-the-sky-ness, the ancient continuing desert-stillness - you have to live there yourself in some time of deep anguish to know how well DESERT can do, to little by little get you to being more of a normal person, quiet-minded, and less "anxious" to be doing something. What you are; not what you can do.

In the course of a few years our homes were like what we wanted them to be. At the time young Ki-Mo-Go came to live in our clan (the young minstrel told of in the opening part of this book), five pretty white Indian homes were in well-separated places in the best reaches of the best one of those big grooves in the rock, down near the water of the stream. We liked white for our stone lodges. We burned lime-rock, and with it made the white-wash we needed. We used that whitening often, so as to keep a good freshness. It was good order, to have the white lodge look clean. We were in the ancient-Indian feeling that things had to be right. Each home must be not what might bring discredit on our old fine clan. How bad it would be, if old Soo-Maa-Hillo would go by, and see a home that had dirty walls to the lodge. We were ever in the feeling that the wise one of our clan, that one who had the best use of the deep mind, was thinking about each one of the homes. We had the feeling that she knew each family well. It was a thing to be trying to have the home the best we could make it. Each boy and girl was that way. That was "Indian", settlement-Indian. The settlement was the thing that showed how fine your

1892

In the clan from which the one good Indian of the Du-Saarte clan (Hual-Pi-Moto) had got his good wife, the young men found young women to be the wives in their homes. Young men from that clan came, and took our girls to be their wives. Years went by. We were in good homes. We had done well in migrating to that place. We had done a good thing when we had got back the old home of the clan, the clan-home the clan had when Sai-Kar-Du was a boy. He had told Wau-Kok stories of how he had done when he was a boy. It was from knowing those stories that Wau-Kok came to know that the place he had found was the place the clan had, many years before.

Two were sad, all those years. Ki-Maa-Ni was not taken by any young man. She was in bad feeling all those years. That is not normal, to have no home of your own, with children in it. She grieved alone all those bad years. Taa-Laa-Go too had no home of his own. How bad that was. The whole clan was sad because of that. They had thought that Taa-Laa-Go would pass by his liking of the daughter of Hual-Pi-Moto. He could not forget her. She would come to him in his dreams.

Ki-Maa-Ni was one who liked to do scouting; she was like her mother in all that. She had taken good training as a scout, so she was almost as good at that as the best ones of the young men. She would go far off in the desert. Usually she was away only a few days.

One time we, my good friend Wau-Kok and I, were talking yet again about that sad thing. "You should go far to find some other clan with whom we could intermarry," he said. We had before that time said that same thing. We had put it off. He was not liking it that I had not done that thing before. "Better go now," he said.

"Would you let me go with you on that long scouting-journey, Waa-Ste?" Taa-Laa-Go asked me.

(How glad I was to hear that. He and I had much in common. He was the one who would be my choice to be the chief-scout, when I gave up that work.) "Would I let you go, Taa-Laa-Go?" I said; "how glad it makes me inside my

1893

mind to know that you would like to do that. I have been dreading that thing ever since I knew it had to be done. How hard it is to go a long journey in dangerous country when you are alone; all the time the strain is on you; you get no good night-rest. You are anxious all the time. If you are continually anxious, you cannot do your best work. With you along - why, it will be fun. Get ready as soon as you can and off we will go."

With what a very different heart I turned back to my lodge. "Laa-Go is going with me, Zo-Ko-To," I called out to my wife. She stood up from what she was doing, there at her small fire. She looked at me. "Is he safe?"

I laughed. "You leave all that to me," I said, "I know a thing or two about how to keep a poor sad sick-hearted boy so busy, his heart will forget the worst of his trouble. He is having it hard here, Zo-Ko-To," I said. "He sees everyone of the clan busy making home grow up. He has no home of his own. He will not give up his Ho-Pek. He sees her in his dreams. She is with him in his mind. He needs to go do hard scouting. He cannot keep his mind from that. It was good here in his new wooded place for a while, but now it may be even worse for him than it would be back in our old settlement in the great canyon, for new young homes are springing up. Do you not see that he needs to be taken entirely away from here for a good while?" (I was very glad that this had come up, for the two Indian woman friends, my Zo-Ko-To and Wau-Kok's Wish-Naa-Ga, would talk that thing over together.)

We would be going as "envoys", as it were, from our little clan to some other clan. This was to be a very special kind of a scouting journey. I lifted that up to the great invisible friend, to great Mo-Kaa, the great wise understanding invisible Mother. Many times, those few days of preparation, I did that. I knew to go to the very wisest person we had in our clan. I must tell you the story of that. Old not-talking Soo-Maa-Hillo was the oldest Indian woman in our clan. She was very old. No one knew how many centuries old she was. No one would ask her that, of course. We knew that she knew even when our old crippled chief, Sai-Kaar-Du

1894

was born. She knew all the important stories the old minstrel of our clan used to tell, before he died (at the time of the migration from the region of the drained-out great salt sea). How deprived I, the young minstrel of the clan was, all those years - because old wise-woman Soo-Maa-Hillo would not talk. (That was one of the best things that ever happened to me, for not being able to tell the old stories at any clan-gathering, I had to get new ones. Doing that for many years did something very important to me: I got so I could get back things from our former cycles of my own past life. If Soo-Maa-Hillo had been normal all those years, I might not have made that good growth, that cycle of my life.)

It was evening. The old Indian woman had chosen as the place of her home a secluded place up out of the gorge, not very far from the big spring that was in a wide green bushy place. It was good for gardens there. It was the place where clearings had been made for some of our necessary gardens. For old Soo-Maa-Hillo, for her special need, that was the only place in the whole pagus for her, for the only clay we had was there in that place. Soo-Maa-Hillo was much interested in making fine things out of clay, clay such as only she knew how to separate out, temper, and mix. We had in our own home a very thin "skillet" made of fired clay that Zo-Ko-To's mother had got from old Soo-Maa-Hillo, when she (Zo-Ko-To's mother) was first married. You, if you could see that old thing now, might think it was of metal; (it looked like old bronze.) How tough were all the things she made. How easily she made her things. Some Indian child would happen there, where the old silent much wrinkled Indian woman would be slowly doing something with some of her mixed clay. The old Indian woman would seem not to see that a child had come. In about three or four days, some boy would come to the home of that small Indian child, and give a nice little package to the Indian mother. In delight, and good expectation, that Indian woman would open slowly that little package. Even the wrapping-thing would be some pretty thing old Soo-Maa-Hillo had made with her own old very skillful hands. If any girls were there at that time, they

1895

would crowd around to see that. It would be some tiny miniature of something that would delight that Indian child a few days before had gone to visit the old lone Indian great grandmother. Having no children of her own, she was grandmother to all the children of the clan. She liked to make miniatures of the little-people. How the many children loved the very old silent Indian woman. What awe she always made come in the hearts of even the older men, when she would appear. We had her as the one to go to - if it was a very hard complicated matter. Wau-Kok was young for the work chiefs have to do. He was wise enough to make good use of what the old Wise-One would get him to see down into. Wau-Kok would go there to her camp. Of course you did not talk to her. With your trouble in your deep mind and heart, you went there and stayed awhile. How strange that was; you always felt better in your heart and mind from doing that. In some way, if that was a problem that you really needed to have clearness about there, great invisible Mo-Kaa would do something that would give you the help you needed. In that way though she did not ever talk, she was an important councellor for the clan. Though she was a woman, the Indian men went to her for help. (You should know that in very ancient times, when age had well matured the person, the being of the other sex did not matter.)

That evening when I got to the camp of the old Indian woman, she was doing a thing I had never before noticed her do, roasting big sunflower seeds. She offered me some.

She grew grave when I had been there a short while. Then, much to my surprise, she got up from there, and walked quickly away. I knew that she was offended at me; I felt that. How strange that was. Of course I could do nothing about that, so I went home. "What was it?" I asked myself again and again that next day. She was without doubt offended. I had gone there with that special mission in my mind. Of course she knew that we were trying to do something about that whole important matter. Not till the fourth day after that evening was the matter cleared up in my mind. My boy, Hee-De brought me one of those little packages. I was

1896

at home in our camp. It was not yet dark. I gave the little thing to my youngest girl to open, supposing that that was something the old woman had made for my little girl. It was a larger miniature than she usually made. It was a good likeness of my own wife. In a flash I saw that was a message to me. She had felt put out, that time, when she had in her mind seen into why I had come there to her, put out that I had gone to her about such a matter as that was, instead of to my own wise wife. In a moment that misunderstanding was cleared up.

In a feeling of relief, and wanting to get back at her, in my mannish way, I got some common coarse mud, mixed it up a little, and made a rude queer old man with it. I made the queer face of him turned, so that he was looking back. I gave it to my boy and told him to take it to the old woman. When he came back after awhile, he said that she had laughed and had tried to hit him with that thing. (The idea of that was that she had misunderstood why I had gone to her; I had gone to her not for the reason she had supposed, but to have her show me what kind of a husband she herself wanted me to bring back to her.)

All this about the old Indian woman knowing what was in the other's mind, will seem not so to the people of these times. I can do nothing about that. If you like to do that, argue yourself out of any belief in these things I write.

We got a very early start. We did not yet know which direction we would go. I was not bothered by that, for I well knew that I would get the guidance I would need. We went up onto the desert (at the place where we had come down into our pagus, the first time of our coming there). We went along a good distance, so as to be away from our own people. It was early in the morning. How still it was, there on the wild desert. We liked that. We were about to set out on what might be a very dangerous very long hard journey. We liked the good feeling of that. That was real Indian doing. "The harder it was - the more good challenge there was to it." We ancient Indians did not like to have things "made easy" for us.

I went up to the top of the ridge, at that place where we

1897

were. The white alkali desert was there to the southward, that other side of the long desert ridge. We were hoping that we would not have to cross it. I had to get the landmark: in a long journey on the desert, you needed to get a distant peak of some mountain-range to be your high guide, to guide you far in the general direction you would go. I was suddenly rebuked. It came to me that my thought had done wrong - that I had not appreciated that barren alkali part of the great desert there: How good a protection that was to our clan; any Indian scout looking down and seeing (from high up on some distant mountain ridge) the white there, would not be in any wish to investigate farther in that general direction. I saw that thing with a clearer understanding of its value to us, that early morning. (Of course, as chief-scout of our little clan, the problem of good defence from enemies was often in my mind.) I was wanting to show my good feeling toward that bad part of the desert, that early morning, so I said, silently in my mind, the thing I knew to say: "Bo No Kaa" (Be ever our good friend.) That matter was taken care of. (How bad it would be, if we had to set off to go the long hard way across the great wideness of that kind of a desert - if you had offended her.)

I got ready to see if great Ko-Waa would give me the sign I needed, show which direction to set off in. I quieted my deeper purer mind. I went into passive feeling - "any way you show us, great invisible friend, so long as we have your good help." Almost immediately there came into my mind this: "Far far to the southwest," the Indian words for that. I told Taa-Laa-Go.

I had the general direction we had to go toward. I had to have a high distant landmark to guide us across the barren desert to the mountains. So I looked the southwest horizon over, to be shown, by some sign, which one of the distinctive mountain-peaks to choose as our guide. I looked that part of the horizon over three times. Not a sign did I get. I looked more to the west. Still no sign was given to me. I looked across to the other side of the alkali desert, there south of us. My eyes went along the horizon. A thing happened; the whole top of one of those mountains lighted up. What a sign

1898

that was. My heart swelled and glowed with that. I knew that we would have good success in our necessary far journey.

We went down from the ridge. We both were feeling the actual presence with us of great invisible Nature. (We knew Nature as both mother, and father. The children's name for the great invisible Mother was a shortened form of her full name. We older ones had got to using in our minds that children's name for her. When we wished to be more formal, her name was the full name, Mo-Kaa-Mo. The name, Mo-Kaa, was almost never spoken in our homes. It was not done that you spoke that name out in words to be taken in by human ears. We knew to keep all that a matter for the "ears" of the deeper purer mind to hear. In my books, books that are for people who do not know these very important facts of human life, I have to come out and say out the precious names of the great invisible Father, and his true Mate. The full name of Father-Nature was "Ko-WAAAA-Mo"). That morning both the invisible Father and the invisible Mother were with us. (If you have been for many years friending intimately with the invisible friends, you know which one of them it is who is with you. You know it if both of them are there.) We were getting the good help of the two of them. They went a way with us that morning. How we were helped by that. We felt that the journey was not any ordinary one (one merely for the getting to know some other clan of friendly Indians). We were silent all day. Not a word did either of us speak, that first day.

In the going the first day of a long hard journey, we did not go very fast. It was not up to the standard "fast-going-of-the-scouts". We needed to get used to the going with the pack, get things to feeling more like they have to feel, if you are to go without any stoppings. (We did no stopping on the desert if we did not have to, for it is a long hard dangerous way, so that going continuously fast till you get all the way across that reach of the desert, if that be possible, is what you try for.) We ancient-Indians were tough; we were like deer, in being able to go continually at a fixed fast rate without stopping.

I could tell the whole story of that long scouting journey,

1899

for I have written that all out in some detail several times. I had to get many things back, from out that cycle of my life. In that long scouting journey things happened that were deeply impressed in my mind. See how all this was with me; I was like any other ordinary person. I had no idea that I had lived before the present life I was living. I had not ever heard that people live more than one time - except that many people believed that when you die, you may have some chance of getting into what is thought of as "Heaven" or maybe it will be "Hell". I was not one who had any thought of delving down into what is called the philosophy of the spirit-world. I had not ever thought that was a good thing to do; I was too busy with my own work to take time for unusual kinds of reading and thinking. I knew of course that there was such a thing as "New-thought" and "Yoga-philosophy" and other kinds of "mysticism". This that I am doing is nothing of that kind. I will not go into any religious matter. That would be much less than courteous. One's relations with the invisible friend are the most private matters there are. How then could I, a stranger, say anything to you about that? I feel very strongly about this matter, for some well-meaning religious persons have, in years past, tried to force their religion on me. I need to say this, here in this place in this book, so that people might know plainly what I am, an ordinary common normal man. What I tell about is normal human life. What I am trying to get persons to wake themselves up to is that daily use of their own deep mind is what they need, along this line of human interest, not any form of "mysticism". It is good wholesome deep practical-psychology, a science that I am interested in. Nature is not limited to mere matters of material-science, of course. If you want to know how to get the measure of the temperature of salt and snow, equal parts, when they are mixed together, you "put that up to Nature", by means of the right experiment. If you want to know what makes you very mad, you put that too up to Nature, in a kind of experiment. In the long-life of you, you have been made very mad by the same kind of things very many thousands of times. What always makes

1900

you, and all other human persons very mad – that is some form of unjustness. That is how we human persons came to have the concept, "justness". All that was worked out, lived out, by thousands of people during the long evolution of the human peoples. Many millions of human people are always made to be very mad by the same kind of bad things that are not right to you, as an individual person. Person – how could Nature be "not-a-person", if everybody gets that kind of knowing from the invisible one? I do not like to seem to "argue" about all this. I wish to help you to think for yourself privately about this very important matter. I, of course, know very well from very much actual personal experience during very many cycles of my own life that Nature is the original pair of parents of all living beings in all the whole world. I, of course, would not think to suggest that you believe this, just because I believe it. You must do your own deep thinking. No other person can do that for you. And no other person's deep thinking will do much good to you if you do not yourself think along with all that, in good willing cooperation with it.

In this book I will tell some of the story of that long scouting-journey, enough of it to serve the purposes of this one of my books. There was very much that I learned that time that I needed to know. I was at a place in the long-life of me when it was necessary for me to think beyond the affairs of the clans-people Indians. I was in the place in the long-life of me when I was ready to move out into wider reaches, in deep thinking into matters of good human living. I needed to know more of how other kinds of people lived, and thought, and believed, and acted. Though of course I did not know it then, I was to do an unusual thing, do a kind of an "experiment" in the matter of living cycles of my own long-life in abnormal clans, so as to know from actual personal experience in those clans how things were in them, know how the persons of the clan actually felt and thought and did. I did that. In the long-life of me I did that. I did not know what I was in for. I had no idea what would happen to me in the long-life of me. Of course when you practise customary breaches of Nature's necessary laws, you go down in

1901

character. You may not be to blame for that. I was not to blame when, as a small child I ate the meat they gave me to eat. (You are not in any awareness of who you are in the long-life of you, when you are still a young child, in that next cycle-of-life you have come up into.) I was in the good care during those very many cycles of my life, of great Ko-Waa and great Mo-Kaa, so that, though I went down in character from what I had been, at my best (far back in ancient times), I was able to climb back upward some, this present cycle of my life. I was not any different this cycle from any other person - till I had gone all the way through several long-drawn-out terrible periods of deep-vastation. So terrible were those periods that I could not have continued to live if I had had to go all the way through in one long period. My whole terrible years-long deep-vastation had to be broken up into several periods, with a rest in between, or I would have died in permanent insanity. My mind was busy with my deep-thinking all that time, and all the years since that time. I have done very much useful deep-thinking this cycle of my life. I have rediscovered a number of very important things in deep practical-psychology that many thousands of thinking persons knew, and made good daily use of, many thousands of years ago. I was an ordinary country-doctor in a small mountain community. I became very much distressed in my mind about that very bad thing that happened to that man Mooney, and his friend, Billings. I could not stay in a State that continued to permit such a terrible thing to go on, year after year after year. I took my wife and two young children and went down into the deserts of western Mexico. I was mildly insane all that time. "I had to get out of my Country." I went down into quiet western desert Mexico. I was in the quieting care of understanding Mother-Nature and Father-Nature. That was the "medicine" they gave to me, in my deep continuing bad anguish, that time. That short stay in Sonora, Mexico, in an old Mexican town down near the southern border of the State of Mexico, was the very thing I needed. For a little while I got entirely away from the terrible maddening great bill-board advertisements of

1902

"Big-Business". In desert Mexico there is none of that. What a relief! Nowhere in all the United States could I have found that. To go along the rude road in the wild dangerous desert and be sure I was, at long last, beyond the maddening advertisements of Big-Business, was the very thing I had to have, at that time, to save me from becoming permanently insane. In an old abandoned Mexican home, in a "has-been" town in Sonora, Mexico, a place where we camped for about a month, I came upon a thing in a small book that my wife had brought along with us in our old automobile. I had not ever come upon that thing before. It was as though I had to go there, far down in desert Mexico (be mildly insane, so that I would do that dangerous hard-to-do thing) – so as to set eyes upon that thing, at just the right psychologic time. I will write that short thing out: "There is an upright stock in a man's own heart that is trustier than any syllogism; and the eyes, and the sympathies and appetites, know a thing or two that have never yet been stated in controversy. Reasons are as plentiful as blackberries; and, like fisticuffs, they serve impartially with all sides. Doctrines do not stand or fall by their proofs, and are only logical insofar as they are cleverly put. An able controversialist no more than an able general demonstrates the justice of this cause."

It was as though I had to go down into western desert Mexico, to find that. I came up out of Mexico with that. I gradually thought my hard way all the way through all the periods of that very terrible time of deep-vastation. My cure started with that. How very much I owe to Robert Louis Stevenson!

One more thing I need to tell about that dangerous Mexican trip. I was in the wise care of the invisible friends day after day after day, or, of course, I would not have even thought to plan to do that thing. My wife does not drive an automobile. Our two children were young at that time. My knowledge of the Spanish language was only enough to let met ask a few simple questions. There were no road-signs at all in the many hundreds of miles of that dry dangerous desert going. We were alone. Many times we were alone

1903

very many miles from any source of water. Gasoline was hard to get. It was a dangerous thing that I did. My wife did not, of course, realize that I was, all that time, mildly insane. I myself did not realize that fact - until some years later; (you yourself do not know that you are insane, if it is mild insanity.)

In one sentence I will sum up all of that: "You are not ever out of the wise understanding care of the invisible friends - if you are not blind in your deeper purer mind."

I will now go on with my story. We had got across the wide bad alkali part of that desert. We had rested up awhile. I had told my young friend, Taa-Laa-Go, that I wanted him to fit himself to be the chief of the scouts in my place, when I quit that work.

Taa-Laa-Go had had good rest. He was young and strong. He was much taken with that idea that he might get to be the chief of the scouts. He had that in his mind already; for I had spoken to him twice before about it. We were alone together. He would have me, the best scout the clan had, to teach him all on that long scouting journey. I saw that he was set up in his mind. I knew that he was taken with that thing. "He would show me that he had it in him to do that work." How he did go all the remainder of the way to the landmark mountain till we got to a place. I will tell you about that.

I had shown Taa-Laa-Go, the morning of that day, the way we would go. (He was for going a different shorter way.) I had been warned that early morning to practise a thing scouts practise when they are in doubt. Taa-Laa-Go, being a young scout thought there was no doubt as to what to do - go on till we got to the base of the landmark-peak of that range of bare desert mountains.

"Pe-Kaa-Ti," that one word, I found in my mind when in the very early morning I had come up out of sleep. I knew that I myself must take back, for the moment, the management of our going. (You will come to know what that ancient-Indian scout-thing was like, as you go along in this story.) My practise of Pe-Kaa-Ti, the morning of that day had got us what seemed a long way out of the way we should have

1904

gone on. It seemed to Taa-Laa-Go that we had made some kind of a mistake. (That was why he could not do that, practise Pe-Kaa-Ti at that time: When you do that, you have to be quiet in the deep mind of you. Taa-Laa-Go, in some doubt about that whole matter, and being young, was not able to get into the deep quiet within him that is necessary for the doing of that thing. He tried for a while to do it.) I had to take over and do it myself. We had come a long way up what turned out to be a long wide gorge-place, the upper end of which was walled in with towering gorge-walls. It seemed, to Taa-Laa-Go, that some mistake had been made. He had thought that he was the one who had made the mistake. (He had been in a kind of a "showing-off" state all that day - so as to show me, the older seasoned hardened chief of the scouts, what he could do. He had tried to get so far ahead of me that I would be out of touch with him. He had tired me more than I should have been tired. I would have camped there for a day or two in that good place had it not been that trying to get the best of me had got my spunk up so that I wished to take some of that out of him, give him more than he would like.) It was because I knew that he was in some doubt and because I wanted him to know that I could stand as much hard going as he could, that I said to him that morning: "Lead on, young scout!" He had not expected that. He had expected that we would camp a few days in that good place (for he had got good water by digging deep in the sand.) He was very tired. He knew what I meant when I gave him that order. He well knew that he had got me to want to show him the results of his own boyishness. He had to do what I, the chief of the scouts, ordered. He was too tired to get any help from that ancient practise of Pe-Kaa-Ti. He tried long to do it. Not a sign could he get.

"I am very sorry, Waa-Ste," he said. "I was foolish all day yesterday. I am too tired, I suppose. You will have to get us out of this bad fix I got us into."

I said nothing. I practised Pe-Kaa-Ti. When you do that, you quiet yourself within. Do that first, then lift all that up to Ko-Waa and await, passively. In good reliance upon the great invisible friend, you look near about you - for the

1905

sign you know you will get. I did that. Almost immediately my eyes saw movement low down in front of us. I looked there. It was the nose of a small lizard. We were too near him to suit him, but - "Who are you?" There was that about the little lizard-person; you felt that was the question in the small mind of him. You felt that not in ten thousand years before that time had any event (like the event we two Indians were that morning) happened there, in that desert-still bare-rock place. He was very deliberate. He looked up us two Indians from out the two small black eyes of him, wondering.

"Not even coyotes," the small lizard finally decided. "I'll chance it, venture out a little." Out a short way up around the rounded edge of the gigantic slab of standing-on-edge bare rock he came. Again he stopped, looking up into the faces of us two serious-faced grateful Indians. "I believe I like them," the lizard-person decided. "I see no reason why I should not go on about my business: The air seems friendly. I will keep my wits about me. I am a very quick one if the enemy thinks to make a quick jump to catch me. Who can run up steep places of the bare rock as quickly as I can? Here goes; I will do that." A considerable way up the steep slope of the rock the little lizard went. He was too full of curiosity to not stop again, when he knew he was safe, a good distance above the heads of those queer "tall-people". He turned the front part of his body a little so as to get a good view, while he stopped there a small while, looking wonderingly down. Again he filled his small eyes with the sight of us two Indians. He did that thing repeatedly as he went deliberately up the considerable way to the top of the great sloping slab of bare rock. He disappeared from our sight up there.

We were in some awe as we had watched that, for was that not the very invisible friend himself (in the guise of a small lizard-person), showing us which way to go to get out of that gorge, and on our way?

We sat down there. How good that place was. I knew that Taa-Laa-Go was sorry for what he had done. I took off my pack, and leaned it up against that steeply-sloping

1906

great giant of a slab. I was about to speak to Taa-Laa-Go, when he did a thing that saddened me; he did that thing involuntarily. I knew right away that, yet again, he had been having a hard time in his very lonely mind. He had, by that little thing, all unwittingly let me see some of the deep old anguish he had to carry all the time, hiding it down in the privacy of his own mind. The little thing he did was to sigh a small almost not-heard sigh. All in a small moment my whole mood toward him was changed. How deeply sorry for him I was.

We remained camped there in that good place one hand of days. I knew that was a very important time in the long hard journey we were in the beginning of. I knew just what Taa-Laa-Go had been thinking while we were getting that good help from the ancient Pe-Kaa-Ti scout-thing. It was yet another of the things he blamed himself for. "I - what I did yesterday - get so very tired that I could not do that necessary scout-thing. How can I ever get so I can be the chief-scout?" That very slight sigh gave me the look I needed to get deep into his suffering heart. Of course I said nothing. He thought we were to be there resting up only one or two days. Maybe he wondered why I stayed on there, day after day. I well knew the deep value of the strange stillness of that kind of a far wild desert place. (We were nearly all walled in there with high vertical walls of smooth bare rock. We had come a long way up into what was a narrowing great gorge. We had got to the head of that great gorge. It was a place an Indian would choose to keep serious vigil.) We talked not at all, those days. We both went apart from each other. I did not once see Taa-Laa-Go till it was the time for us to go on our way. We would go for necessary water. Neither one of us ate any food those days. We both slept most of that time. (Sleep gives the deeper purer mind of you the chance it needs to show you the important things you need to know.)

Why did I "waste" those days? We were at the beginning of a journey that might keep us from home a whole year. I must get you to do some thinking for yourself privately. We two were in what we thought of as being the

1907

work of being friends. Though I had my obligations to my clan, and was sent by the clan on an important journey, I was, too, a friend of young Taa-Laa-Go. I was in my warm camp-bed, the next morning after the little lizard had shown us the way to get up out of the great gorge. (Though it was a thing that seemed impossible, our getting up out of the deep gorge, up high walls that were in most places nearly vertical, I was not anxious about that matter. I had got help so often from having just such a thing as that happen to me, just after I had practised Pe-Kaa-Ti, that I was sure in my mind that we would find some good way to get on our way without having to turn back, and go the long way back out of the great long dry wide gorge. I was not having that in my mind at all.) I had come to know that there was more trouble in the deep mind of my young friend, Taa-Laa-Go, than I had known about before that time.

I had been in a drowsy state. I was but dimly awake. It was so quiet that you felt that no noise had happened there for a thousand years, or more. You feel things like that, when you are out in some great wide desert-region. I liked the rest I was getting there. I had not known that I was tired. I was full of the plans we leaders of the clan had, for going on with the things that would make better homes for all our families, in the good pagus we had. I had, of course, many different kinds of small troubles in my mind. I was away from all that. I would be away from all that for many months. I felt, in a way, good relief. In my sleep that night, I must have gone down far in my mind, for I knew that my sleep had been deeper than usual. I was not in any anxiety, that morning. I was feeling the deep peace of that quiet mountain region. It was as if I had come there to the very feet of the great mountain to get some of the age-old peace he had in him. "What are mere human things, anyway"? I had some of that feeling in me. In my dim awareness of coming day I had come up into that kind of a mood. Then - "It is no," that phrase was there in my mind. How singular. I came awake with that in my mind. "What does it mean?" my mental-mind asked. I knew it was some kind of a sign that had been given by my deep mind up into my less-deep one.

1908

I had no link in my mind that would connect those words with my own thinking. I was not trying to explain it to myself. Things like that often happen to one. The deep mind is submental; all the time when you are asleep things go on there. We are that way, part submental, and part mental. What is mental you are aware of. What is submental you are not aware of. There is a place in between what is submental, and what is mental. I know no good name for that very important psychologic "place". One is "in a drowsy state". That is good enough. You know what that is. I was, very long ago, not even thinking that there were mental states, and submental ones. We were not "philosophers" in those times. We made use of what we had.

In ways like that we passed the days of that period of rest. We two Indians were in good friending, the one with the other, though we were not near each other as to the bodies of us. It must have been something that was going on in the troubled mind of Taa-Laa-Go, not something from deeper down in my own submental mind that got that thing said out into the mental mind of me that early morning. Those days were days of trouble in the mind of young Taa-Laa-Go. Of course I would not want to know anything of all that. It was for me, the more mature one, to know when I should move on from there. I came to know that Taa-Laa-Go needed to go through a long series of things in his deep mind. He had lost the girl who was to have been his mate. We were going to some clan where there might be girls who might be what he would like. He was in a submental way, all in doubt about how his life was to be. Would he marry some other woman? How could he live the life of an unmarried person all the years of a whole cycle of life? How abnormal that would be. But - Ho-Pek. He could not forget his loved Ho-Pek. I knew it when it was the time to go from there.

We got up to the top of that great slab of rock, the one up which the lizard had gone. When we got up there with our packs (by using our good hair-ropes), we found the hole the lizard had gone into. We cleared out the loose broken rock from that place. We found that the other great standing-on-

1909

edge slab that was up there was the cover for a long steep cave-place. We went, in the dark, a long way going on our hands and feet up a steep slope. We were behind a sloping slab of rock. We got up out of that gorge-end through that steep place. We came out, high up, to look off down into the end of another narrow gorge (one up which Taa-Laa-Go would have come from far off on the rocky approach to the mountain if I had not done what the invisible friend had shown me to do, practise Pe-Kaa-Ti).

I will not tell you all of that long story. How many times I have worked on that one of the Indian stories I had to get back from out that cycle of my life. I have to make each one of my books be a not-too-long book. I have told enough of how we went as we went the long hard wearing journey. We had many narrow escapes. We would be so tired sometimes that we would not be alert enough to get the slight signs the invisible friend would give us - we would have to get a terrible sign, one that would make us go much farther out of our course than would have been necessary if we had to the first little sign. We had to go a very long way eastward, before we got the sign that told us to go westward. We knew that the region we had to go to was far to the southwest of of our home-region. We had to find the distant settlement, two months' journey from our home, by using our own deeper minds in the way all wise ancient-Indian scouts used to do: I will take you on in this story, skip ahead to the time we were in the home of the old minstrel of the big clan we had got to, far away from our own small settlement.

How very different that clan was from what we had expected to find. We had thought that we would find a small clan something like our own clan. We had not heard that there were big rich clans like that one was. We were in a home in the old settlement. Homes, many homes, were all about us in that wide well-watered valley. We had looked down upon it from a distant high rocky ridge. We had been amazed at what we saw. We could not easily believe what we saw. How great were the gardens. How green the whole plain was. We had seen that they had made a channel so big and long that they had got all of the small river to go in it; they used all of the water of their river to water the great expanse of gardens. "How can they need so very much food?" we asked ourselves, as we got the meaning of all that we were looking at into our minds.

"o y ya o y ya lal lal lal la la la". In my bed, that early morning I heard that. It was far away so that it came only faintly to me. I heard that and other distant noises. I knew that already the early-morning work of that great clan had begun. I was feeling that it was the beginning of another one of those hot-region days. Here they would have to work long into the heat of the desert-region day. I was wishing I was back home in our own small settlement. "Will any young men from such a great clan as this one is want as their mates our kind of young woman?" I asked myself. I was in "a room", a rich private place of the home of the old fat minstrel. We both, Taa-Laa-Go and I, had the same room together. (We had been out in the open for months. We would much rather have camped by ourselves in some place where we could have had some privacy.) He was a minstrel. He was so "courteous" to us that he did not feel in his mind what we ourselves would much rather have done. We were not liking that great settlement. These things that we had come upon were of course, signs. We felt what the signs got us to feel. (You are not always mentally aware of the sign: many signs given to you are signs that do something to the submental mind of you, your mental mind not taking notice of all that, they do things that put you into the mood you need to be in.)

"We need to go to the place where they wash in the morning," I thought to myself. I got up from the very soft thick sleeping mat. My left foot was sore because of a piece of cactus needle that had gone in deep and had broken off. Both Taa-Laa-Go and I had trouble with those things. We wore nothing on our feet in those times. Ordinarily no wounds ever came on our tough feet. The old minstrel had noticed that we were limping. He knew us for strangers because in the distance he saw two Indians who were walking with a limp. That had been the evening before.

1911

He, the old minstrel, was the first one of those Indians to whom we came when we got near to the lodge that was nearest to us as we approached the big settlement. That old minstrel knew us for strangers because we wore nothing on our feet. In that great South-country many small cactuses grew. It was impossible sometimes to avoid stepping where the small cactus-needles were. You would not know any cactus was there. Some places that you might go in at night would be all covered with many small loose sharp cactus-needles. We were Indians from the North. We had not ever been in the regions where Indians had to wear sandals. We were known for strangers by the fact that we had no sandals on our feet.

My left foot was sore and there was no way to get the small piece of cactus-needle out. I had been bothered a good deal by that thing. Of course I knew that was some kind of a sign from the invisible friend. That first morning after we had arrived at that big settlement my foot was so bad that I would have hopped to the place of washing-up, if it had been in a small settlement. There it seemed to me that I must do more like a dignified person would do. Though my foot hurt much, I walked without any limp to that place. It was the very thing. That putting the weight of my body on that place opened up the small abscess that had formed there. A good amount of pus came out and I was hoping that the piece of cactus-needle had come out with the pus. I was doing what I could do for my sore foot when the old minstrel came. He saw what had happened.

"You are too sore in that foot to go on it," he said. "I will send for one of our young men who knows how to get the needles out. In a few days your foot will be in a better condition. I am sorry I did not know how bad your foot is. It should have had good care last evening."

In three days time I was in the bad state that infection causes. That young man had thought that he had to cut into my sore foot and do much searching for that small piece of cactus-needle. He was one who would not quit till he had done what he was supposed to do. He did not find the small bit of cactus-needle. It probably had come out with the

1912

pus, he thought, afterwards. He had made a small matter be a serious one.

How bad the old minstrel felt. I had to stay on my bed in that room for two hands of days. How bad I was feeling all that time that I was causing so much trouble to the two old Indians. They would take care of me themselves, not give that work over to any young person. They were both old and fat, so fat that what they did for me was work to them. They were not used to doing any work of any kind. All these things, and many more things, I got to know, during that time when my foot was swollen and in a bad condition. It was fortunate that they let me do for my foot myself, after they knew how bad the thing done by that young Indian was. When they knew that I was the medicine-man of my own clan, they ceased trying to get me to have their own medicine-man take care of my sore foot. Taa-Laa-Go got for me the herbs I needed and made for me the medicine I had to have. It was not as bad after the first three days; and I knew that I would be able to take the swelling down in a month or more of careful doing with it. I was not in as good condition as I would have been if they would have let met go far out somewhere where I could have had a camp alone by myself.

Taa-Laa-Go was with me for two hands of days. He saw that we would need to find a smaller clan than that one was, for our small clan to intermarry with. He had talked with some scouts of that big clan; he had got from them the scout-signs by which it would be possible to go southward to the settlement of a small clan. We decided that he should go on alone while I was getting well of my bad leg.

How much there is to tell. I could make a book of all that we learned, while we were on that one long dangerous scouting-journey. I will tell of a very bad terrible thing that happened. It will be enough to let you know the little that you now need to know of yellowlegs badness. In each one of my books there is a good purpose that I must make clear, in good strong ways. If I let myself go off too much into the interesting side-stories, I confuse the reader who needs to get cleared up in his own mind some important

1913

matters. It is a difficult thing that I am trying to do - get some thinking persons to go deeper in thinking out the important problems of human life, so that they will get so they will see and know surely that the ancient clan way of living is the only way that is normal, and is the only way that can be permanently satisfying. I must not let mere interesting stories in my books get the reader off from the things the book is written to make clear. I must, of course, make my books as interesting as I can make them be. In a good number of short books I hope to tell something of the life that was lived very far back in the ancient times when clans were the governments of all of the best people everywhere. One great departure from that had already got off to a very extensive growth.

My mind was full of the deep trouble while I was badly disabled with that unnecessary sickness of that leg. (Had that young man not got some ideas of "efficiency" from a Yellowlegs "Boss" of the affairs of that rich clan of settlement-Indians, I would have got well of that injury to my foot in a few hands of days. I was a guest in the home of one of the important persons of that clan; so, of course, I had let that old minstrel do the thing he felt was the courteous thing to do. I did not at first tell him that I myself was the medicine-man of our own clan. Had I had any idea of what the "trained" young man would do, of course I would not have let him be sent for.)

In the days of my being compelled to be there in that room on that sleeping-mat, I got from the old minstrel much about how things were in that big clan. Of course you "do not ask questions" at a time like that. All that the old minstrel told me - that was "the natural thing", in that big settlement. I got a little about those Yellowlegs people at the first when that young Indian was trying to get to find the small piece of cactus-needle in my sore foot. He said to me: "My Yellowlegs teacher told me that I should try to get the thing out that caused the sickness of the place; you might get a very bad leg from leaving that small thing in." He had been merely "trained" for that work; he was no medicine-man. He did not make use of the deep mind in

1914

his work. How much I was to find out about those powerful efficient knowing pushing-all-out people, there in that settlement. I did not ask the old minstrel anything about the affairs of his clan; that was not done in those times. I heard what was talked. I saw what was being done. When I got so I could walk out, the minstrel would take me on short walks, so as to show me how things were done in their clan. I was astonished at what I saw. I was so astonished, one day, when I saw that they had extensive gardens all in sugar-cane, that I asked the old minstrel: "Why do you have so much of this?"

He sat down in the shade of a big nut tree. (It was hot for that was desert-region. The much water in that favored little fertile valley made the heat all the harder to bear, for the air was sultry. We were both glad to sit down and rest awhile. The old minstrel would carry with him a woman-kind of a thing, a fan. He was that kind of an Indian, an old respected rich one of the clan. In that clan of ancient-Indians the clan idea had become a thing more of mere form than of actual fact. The thing there was to get to be an old respected waited-on man, or woman, one who did not ever work. All the best homes were in the hands of the most influential ones of the clan. Those best homes had grown, had grown at the expense of the many small meager homes of the common Indians, the younger Indians who had to do all of the work for the old rich owners of most of the good land of that whole valley. The way they did there was for the younger men to work on the "estate" of some one of the old influential owners of the land. He, the younger man, was supposed to be getting his start up toward what the old ones were enjoying. The poor families either had small lodges on the land of some rich owner, or they had a small home-place up out of the valley. All of the water was the property of the relatively few old rich families. Those poor families that had their homes all to themselves had to carry water for home use, or dig a well, and draw their water up out of it. That was something like we have it now, in these times. It was very far back in ancient times that the plan of having poor people work for you was easily accomplished by getting control of all the best land. That way of doing got started very long ago; that is no mere recent way of doing. That is very much against the ancient clan way of doing.)

I have come upon this thing. It happened to come into the story at this place. I did not see that thing in former renderings of this part of my story: I did not see that I should go into the thing. Now, in this much shorter rendering, I see that I must tell something about the "land-question". That was one of the things the ancient Yellowlegs people "solved" in such a way that they easily got the use of millions of Indians who were not their bond-slaves. They, the Yellowlegs people, used very many thousands of bond-slaves. They were very "thorough" in all that they did, those efficient Yellowlegs people. The government was one great powerful centralized government for all the many thousands of Yellowlegs people. They had a thought-out plan for everything. The idea of "standardization" was used very much by those people. They used the "caste" way of doing the much work of all the very large settlements. Each kind of work was done by a special caste of workers; the people were in separate "strata", you might say; all the upper "strata" rested down on the slaves. Everything was in the control of the chief officers of the great centralized government. They had a very highly-respected group of customs that were what now we would call a religion. How very terrible that religion was! The government and that religion, were one and the same thing. Priests were the officers of the government. You were disobeying the GREAT GOD if you were even slack in some of your ordinary duties. "Priests", the officers of the "federal" government, were everywhere. Very many of them were among the many slaves, disguised as slaves. They were very "thorough" in all that they did. They believed that it was their mission to manage well the affairs of all the common people everywhere. Believing that, and feeling that they were "chosen-ones", chosen by the great Gods of the glorious UNDERWORLD, they worked hard at that.

(to be continued in next issue)

1916

THE HIDDEN WORLD

HERE NOW ARE the first TWO VOLUMES in a continuing series originally released by Publisher Ray Palmer in the 1960s, and hereby reprinted for the Serious Student of the Shaver and Inner Earth Mysteries!

**TO COME IN TOTAL 16 BOOKS, OVER 3200 PAGES AND ALMOST TWO MILLION WORDS!
14 MORE VOLUMES TO COME!**

HIDDEN WORLD NUMBER ONE:
The Dero! The Tero! And The Battle For Good And Evil Underground!

Here, in over 200 pages, is the beginning of The Shaver Mystery!

· Shaver hears the tormented voices coming from below.

· Readers question his sanity when he describes entering the caves of the ancients.

· He describes in detail the plunder of our planet by extraterrestrials in ancient times, and the lost continents of Lemuria and Atlantis.

· Shaver "proves his case" by revealing an ancient alphabet he calls "Mantong."

· Captured by the Dero from ancient races, the stem and mech machines cause utter chaos on surface dwellers, Wars, murder and horrific accidents are caused by the "evil ones."

THIS RARE REPRINT ONLY $25.00

HIDDEN WORLD NUMBER TWO:
The Masked World of Richard Shaver

The epic underground saga continues in roughly 190 pages of the nightmarish dealings with Inner Earth dwellers.

· A dark cloud hangs over the Earth as the subsurface mutants kidnap and torture humans, even performing cannibalistic acts upon their flesh.

· A series of airplane crashes carrying well-known celebrities can be blamed on the demented robot-like Dero.

· Shave reveals the secrets of "Growing A Better Man."

· Voices in the night torment readers of Shaver's tales as they confirm many of his claims.

THIS RARE REPRINT ONLY $25.00

SPECIAL OFFER: Both volumes One and Two of THE HIDDEN WORLD for the combined price of just $39.95. Please add $5.00 S/H to the total order.

Explore The Shaver and Inner Earth Mysteries

**Global Communications
Box 753 · New Brunswick, NJ 08903**

www.ingramcontent.com/pod-product-compliance
Lightning Source LLC
Chambersburg PA
CBHW081222170426
43198CB00017B/2690